How Corruption Affects Social and Economic Development

The Dark Side of Political Economy

HOW CORRUPTION AFFECTS SOCIAL AND ECONOMIC DEVELOPMENT
The Dark Side of Political Economy

Volume I

Rupert Hodder

With a Foreword by
Miriam Defensor-Santiago

The Edwin Mellen Press
Lewiston•Queenston•Lampeter

Library of Congress Cataloging-in-Publication Data

Hodder, Rupert.
  How corruption affects social and economic development : the dark side of political economy / Rupert Hodder ; with a foreword by Miriam Defensor-Santiago.
    v. <1> ; cm.
  Includes bibliographical references and index.
  ISBN-13: 978-0-7734-5299-2
  ISBN-10: 0-7734-5299-0
  1. Political corruption. 2. Political corruption--Economic aspects. I. Title.
  JF1081.H63 2007
  338.9--dc22

                                                    2007040627

  hors série.

A CIP catalog record for this book is available from the British Library.

The Edwin Mellen Press
Box 450
Lewiston, New York
USA 14092-0450

The Edwin Mellen Press
Box 67
Queenston, Ontario
CANADA L0S 1L0

The Edwin Mellen Press, Ltd.
Lampeter, Ceredigion, Wales
UNITED KINGDOM SA48 8LT

Printed in the United States of America

338.9 Hod.

For dad (November 25, 1923 - September 12, 2006)

He taught me how to live, and showed me how to meet death. No man could give more to his son; no son could ask more of his father.

They that have the power to hurt and will do none,
That do not do the things they most do show,
Who, moving others, are themselves as stone,
Unmovèd, cold, and to temptation slow;
They rightly do inherit heaven's graces
And husband nature's riches from expense;
They are the lords and owners of their faces,
Others but stewards of their excellence.
The summer's flower is to the summer sweet,
Though to itself it only live and die;
But if that flower with base infection meet,
The basest weed outbraves his dignity:
For sweetest things turn sourest by their deeds;
Lilies that fester smell far worse than weeds

William Shakespeare

TABLE OF CONTENTS

FOREWORD

In this book, Rupert Hodder puts together a thoughtful and stimulating debate on the problem of corruption. It provides a concise, balanced, and lively introduction to corruption's meaning, extent, causes and solutions. Yet it also takes the reader much further into a scholarly, intriguing, and really quite original understanding of corruption.

Corruption, he argues, is better understood as a term given to all kinds of behaviour which, if they are to be comprehended, need to be left and analysed in context rather than abstracted and analysed as 'corruption-the-phenomenon'. When this is done, we begin to see that corruption is simply one expression of social change, but one that goes right to the heart of human nature. Behavior which we might often describe as corrupt reflects basic shifts in the way we see the world, other people, and our place in that world.

No attempt is made to duck the issue - this *is* a moral question, and an important one at that. There is no place for cultural or moral relativism here; but neither are there simple rights and wrongs. We cannot understand goodness or propriety unless we understand and experience in ourselves immorality and impropriety. In fact, an attempt to lay out sets of instructions in morality and propriety, let alone to compel others to follow these codes, starves us of an appreciation of morality and will lead us into orthopraxy (a kind of obsessive political, bureaucratic and procedural correctness).

This suffocating behavior, increasingly evident in the western world, is pernicious exactly because it prevents society from discovering and knowing morality intimately. At least the kind of personalism - a self-centred instrumentalism - which is often thought to characterize corruption in developing countries leaves open a way to a true appreciation of virtue.

Clearly, solutions to corruption must go beyond attempts to uncover wrongdoing and shut down opportunities, and may not be that difficult or costly. The everyday routine operation of everyday organizations - such as family businesses and even governmental and bureaucratic organizations - may act as agents for change. If we can identify and understand those practices in society which are already stimulating more positive attitudes and images of self and world, then we may be able to encourage further what is already underway, and do so without diverting too much energy, time or money from existing government priorities. And if we can link these hotspots together and help them to support and encourage each other, it may be possible to achieve a tipping point - a point at which corruption is spontaneously squeezed out of society.

But where and what are those hotspots, how might they be encouraged, and how do we show that these kinds of measures work and deserve serious attention? There are plenty of more high profile and direct attacks on corruption which are more likely to capture interest and money. Again Rupert Hodder tackles the problem head on, and sketches out ways in which the more philosophical elements of his suggested analytical approach can be tied into the gritty realities that have to be faced on the ground. Whether and how this works out in practice in the Philippines is a question the second volume will examine.

This is a thorough, interesting, and imaginative work of scholarship which I commend to the reader.

Senator Miriam Defensor-Santiago, Republic of the Philippines.
Chair, Committee on Foreign Relations; PhD (Michigan).

v

ACKNOWLEDGEMENTS

This research is an extension of a project on institutional change supported by the British Academy, and would not have been possible without extended leave to work in the Philippines. Thanks are due to the British Academy for its initial financial support, and to my Faculty (and especially to Professors Neil Roberts and Richard Gibbs) for the time they gave me. In Manila, where the fieldwork and much of the writing is being done, I have many people to thank. A more comprehensive list of acknowledgements will appear in the second volume. For the moment, however, I would like to express my gratitude to Consuela, Tessie and Obeth who never fail to deliver; to An Ka-Pei whose faith seems endless; to Senator Miriam Defensor-Santiago; to Senator Ramon B. Magsaysay Jr.; to Senator Jinggoy Estrada; to Senator Aquillino Q. Pimentel Jr. (Senate Minority Floor Leader) and his Chief-of-Staff Attorney Frank Navarette; to Attorney Rafael G. Hipolito (Acting Director, Bureau of Resident Ombudsman); and to Father Jack Carroll, former director of the Institute on Church and Social Issues Incorporated, Ateneo de Manila University Campus. But above all, I would like to thank San: as ever, *diliko mahimo ning tanan kung wala ka!*

Manila
March 12, 2007

INTRODUCTION

This book is the first of two volumes that together consider how we might analyse, explain, understand and solve corruption. In this first volume, the discussion on corruption's effects, causes, and solutions, is set at a fairly general level. It argues that acts regarded as corrupt are best examined as part of the broader organic and dimensional context in which they occur, and as a reflection of the way those who take part in, or eschew, corruption envisage their social world and treat their social relationships. Central to this examination, is an understanding of a play of representations, practice and attitudes. *Representations* describe an individual's construction of self and self's place in that world. Representations inform our practice, enabling us to operate physically within the natural and social worlds and to organise particular instances of our everyday lives. *Practice* is used to refer to the practice of our social relationships, and describes how we behave. The term *attitude* describes the extent to which we view and treat our relationships as either *personal* or *affective*. By a *personal* attitude we mean the extent to which we think of relationships as instruments or a means to an end. By an *affective** attitude we

---

*Weber uses the term 'affectional action' to describe action driven by emotion; and, indeed, the terms 'affective' and 'affect' more commonly refer to an association between emotions and desire on the one hand, and action and thought on the other. There is, in this meaning, something of a distinction to be made between thought (and action) and emotional states of mind. In view of this more customary usage, it is worth emphasizing that we understand 'affect' and 'affective' rather differently in these pages. As we have said, they are taken to describe the treatment of relationships (together with ideas, emotions, values, institutions, organisations, rules, roles, processes, laws, procedures and conventions) *as if* important and significant in their own right or, in other words, *as if* absolute.

mean the extent to which we think of our relationships *as if* they are absolute – *as if* they are important in their own right. At the heart of the play (or mutual influence) among representations, attitudes and practice, lie shifts in attitude. As instrumentalism rises, our views (or representations) of 'self' and 'others' become more negative, and alienation deepens. This shift (towards the instrumentalism or the personal) is also associated with growing authoritarianism or nihilism, and with more negative views (or representations) of the world. Conversely, as instrumentalism falls, views of 'self' and 'others' strengthen, while levels of alienation fall. Associated with this shift (towards the affective) are greater tolerance and more positive views of the polity and bureaucracy. These shifts have a profound influence on the quality of institutions. A shift towards the personal creates uncertain, introverted, poorly focussed and weak institutions that are more prone to corruption. A shift towards the affective produces more professional, focussed, efficient and robust organisations.

The solution to corruption - to encourage shifts in attitude (towards the affective) and alterations in representations of the social world - is comparatively straightforward, at least when viewed from the safety of an armchair. Elsewhere (Hodder, 2006) we have argued that the ordinary day-to-day operations of political, bureaucratic and economic organizations - even those that are weak and uncertain, or rigid and authoritarian - appear to produce among their staff changes in attitudes, representations and practice that amount to the growth of professionalism. Through the social and civic lives of staff outside the institution, these changes influence wider society where other positive stimuli, through those same channels, find their way back into the institution. Such changes occur all the time but often go unnoticed or unsaid, and are left to whither, precisely because they seem so ordinary and unimportant. Yet they are, we argue, at least as profound as any reforms that are likely to be produced through those institutions' specific functions, or through any policy or legislation they shape or implement. If the institutional arrangements and activities responsible for these changes in attitude, representation, and practice, can be identified and explained, they may provide an effective means of dealing with corruption at minimum economic and political cost.

But all this has the smell of the lamp about it. The difficulties lie, firstly, in communicating and explaining why and how these attitudes and representations work, and how they help us to understand corruption. Secondly, we must demonstrate: that representations, attitudes, and practice, do work in the field in the ways that we say they do; that the prompts or hotspots of change - the organizational arrangements and activities which stimulate more positive attitudes, representations, and practices - are already present and indeed significant; and that the identification and enhancement of these prompts - even though they do not appear to tackle the problem of corrupt behaviour directly - should nevertheless take priority over the more obvious assaults on corruption. If we are to address this second group of difficulties, then we must develop ways that enable us: to unpick the play between our representations of the world, our attitudes to social relationships, and our practice; and to do so with reference to specific instances in the field.

This first volume begins to address the first set of difficulties - to outline possible ways disaggregating representations, attitudes and practice. The second volume takes up these ideas and examines: how, in the case of the Philippines, they operate in field; whether we can indeed identify and encourage hotpots; and whether this will have the effects we intend.

CHAPTER 1
Definition, Extent and Effects

1.0 Introduction: definition and description

At first sight a definition of 'corruption' would not seem to be controversial. The word is used as a synonym 'evil', 'moral depravity', 'rotten' and 'putrid'; it may also mean 'to destroy' or 'to make unreliable'. It is used more often to describe the perversion of behaviour, procedures, beliefs, values, institutions, personalities or entire societies from what is held to have been their proper, true, genuine or natural state. And it is readily understood as a willingness to act dishonestly in return for money or some other gain. Corruption, then, carries the sense that one is putting the interests of self before the interests of a wider body.

There are many attempts to bring more precision to the word corruption. For Nye (1967, p.419) the word is used to describe

> 'behaviour which deviates from the formal duties of a public role because of private-regarding (personal, close family, private clique), pecuniary or status gains; or violates rules against the exercise of certain types of private-regarding influence. This includes such behaviour as bribery (use of reward to pervert the judgement of a person in a position of trust); nepotism (bestowal of patronage by reason of ascriptive relationship rather than merit); and misappropriation (illegal appropriation of public resources for private-regarding uses).'

6

A similar but more concise definition is provided by McMullan (1961, pp. 183-4) who understands a public official to be corrupt if he

> 'accepts money or money's worth for doing something that he is under duty to do anyway, that he is under duty not to do, or to exercise a legitimate discretion for improper reasons.'

Bayley (1970, p.522) favours a still more succinct phrase: the 'misuse of authority as a result of considerations of personal gain, which need not be monetary' - a definition close to the Santhanam Committee Report's (1964) description of corruption as the 'improper and selfish exercise of power and influence attached to public office or to the special position one occupies in public life' (p.5). Other writers however, prefer to understand corruption as behaviour which, for private advantage, harms public interests, and which may also, but not necessarily, offend the rules and conventions of public office (Rogow and Lassell, 1970; Friedrich, 1963).

These two sets of definitions (the former set is often referred to as public-office-centred, and the latter as public-interest-centred) make a distinction of emphasis between actions that are themselves corrupt and those which are corrupt because they have a deleterious effect on public institutions, processes, and procedures. Yet if we are prepared to interpret 'public interest' flexibly, then neither definition appears to be bound by ethical considerations. Both understandings of corruption could, for instance, be applied either to those who pursue democracy and religious freedom in a centralised theocracy, or to those whose actions are helping to undermine a secular and democratic state. The common meaning which these definitions carry, then, is contravention and possible weakening of an established political economy's formal institutions, rules, procedures, processes and conventions. This sense is perhaps best captured by Leff's (1964, p.8) description of corruption as 'an extra-legal institution used by individuals or groups to gain influence over the actions of the bureaucracy. As such, the existence of corruption *per se* indicates only that these groups participate in the decision-making process to greater extent than would otherwise be the case'.

A third set of definitions (market-centred) describes corruption as behaviour which, though it may contravene established rules and amounts to an abuse of office, is nevertheless entirely rational in that it is motivated by a desire to maximise either influence or income or both. Such behaviour is commonly understood as a response to disequilibrium in supply and demand in centralised (usually socialist) allocative bureaucracies (van Klarven, 1970; Tilman, 1968). These market-centred definitions (in comparison with public-office-centred and public-interest-centred definitions) appear to be flavoured more strongly with ideology - that of the primacy of economic rationality.

The qualities and features which the practice of corruption is thought to take on, are numerous enough to have attracted all kinds of taxonomies. Indeed, we might suggest a taxonomy of taxonomies comprising three categories, each cross-cutting or subsuming parts of the other.

(i) The first category – means – describes the means of inducement or the kinds of rewards or items exchanged. This includes, for instance, traditional corruption (such as nepotism and the exchange of gifts) and modern corruption (financial payments).

(ii) The second category - spheres - describes very general classes of activity in *Where.* which corruption is present. The most obvious classes are politics, business, economics, and bureaucracy. Others may include public, private, internal, external, domestic and international. Khan's (1998, p.18) useful and straightforward definition – that of 'the violation of the formal rules governing the allocation of public resources by officials in response to offers for financial gain

Khan - good definition in reference to political aspect. Use to support.

or political support' – sets corruption more narrowly[*] within in the realm of political and bureaucratic allocation. Still more precise spheres are also commonly discussed in the literature. These include quite specific, and often rather technical, practices such as the disclosure of privileged information and embezzlement. Another - and this is a one which falls within the broader category of bureaucratic corruption – is the payment of 'speed' money. This refers to payments made to officials to hasten, say, the processing of a licence or a visa application. Yet another sphere is procurement fraud – the selection of contracts and consultants according to criteria other than those of least cost and best quality.

cause

The Asian Development Bank (1998, p.6), on the other hand, weakens the distinction between public and private, arguing that whilst corruption is used most commonly to describe acts within public institutions, it is just as common within the private sector. A better definition, in its view, is

> 'behaviour on the part of officials in the public and private sectors, in which they improperly and unlawfully enrich themselves and/or those close to them, or induce others to do so, by misusing the position in which they are placed.'

Indeed we might make the case that corruption is, almost by definition, the blurring of distinctions among spheres.

EVALUATION

(iii) The third category – scale and depth – describes variations in the extent and seriousness of corruption. This category includes, for instance, corruption that is 'minor' (such as bending minor rules for friends), 'routine' (such as directing contracts or preferment to those who helped to secure votes during an election), and 'aggravated' (such as tolerating organised crime or changing party allegiances in return for money) (Heidenheimer, 1970 a). Also included within scale and depth are classes such as 'level', 'deviation', and 'rents'. The first of these refers to the level (upper or lower) of the beneficiary; the second refers to the degree of

---

[*] Just how narrowly, depends upon how the word 'resources' is interpreted.

deviation (marginal or extensive) from formal duties; and the last, 'rents' (a term used widely in the literature), may be understood as the reward (usually financial) paid by businesses to the state in return for its creation of monopolies and other market distortions which favour businesses with large and protected incomes. These rewards - paid for hidden or thinly disguised concessions - are made over to individuals (such as a government minister or high-ranking bureaucrat) or to institutions (say a political party). The size and complexity of these arrangements tends to imply that corruption is widespread, systematic and deeply ingrained within the political economy. This sense is also carried by 'rent-seeking', and is further emphasised by the phrase 'top-down rent-seeking' - that is, the creation and parcelling out of concessions by a state which may, for that reason, be described as predatory. The term 'bottom-up rent-seeking' (or rent-seeking by society) may imply sporadic, occasional, and uncoordinated corruption. But it need not do so: the power to persuade or compel bureaucrats and politicians to rig the market on a large scale may lie with businesses. In this case, the phrase 'state capture' may be applicable.

'Centralised' and 'decentralised' also convey a feeling of scale. The former describes the organisation of corruption into what is, for all intents and purposes, a one-stop-shop. A single large payment - made to the head of state or to a political party or to a cabinet minister - may be all that is required: doors are then opened, short-cuts revealed, and preferential treatment secured throughout a country without any further payments having to be made. 'Decentralised' corruption, on the other hand, suggests that officialdom is poorly coordinated and less predictable, such that many agreements and exchanges may have to be made. Similar meanings and ideas of scale are also conveyed by terms such as 'systematic' (the involvement of an entire ministry or government) and 'individual' (occasional and sporadic); by 'syndicated' and 'non-syndicated'; 'grand' (corruption that involves large payments, senior officials, and the exercise of influence over important policies or major decisions) and 'petty' (corruption that involves small sums of money, low-ranking officials, and influence over minor processes of the polity and bureaucracy).

2.0 Problems

Although it might seem that we have managed to sharpen up both our definition of corruption and our descriptions of the forms it takes, there are a number of problems with these kinds of understandings. A consideration of these problems soon makes it apparent that a meaning of corruption is not quite as straightforward as we may have first thought.

Propriety and relativity

(i) The first problem is an understanding - and agreement - of the nature of the thing that is being corrupted. What is the 'proper' state of affairs that is being corrupted? In particular, are there universal standards of 'good', 'proper', and 'correct", or are such judgements only relative? Too many definitions, it might be said, reflect notions of convention, morality, and propriety that are assumed, quite wrongly, to be universal. The United Kingdom, for instance, appears to be much less corrupt than many other parts of the world, and there are various measures that seem to bear this out (see section 3.0 below). But if we hold that trade (exchange for profit) and the legal, political and social frameworks which together form 'capitalism' in a democratic state are inherently wrong, then the UK's formalised system now appears merely to legitimise behaviour and actions that are unfair and unjust and cause most people to be un-free. Through this critical - some would say cynical and conspiratorial – perspective, all kinds of questions about the UK emerge. How is it that ministers may order its citizens to sacrifice their lives in war without being honest with them about the reasons for that war? Why should the prime minister and leaders of the oppositions in the UK be so concerned to win the backing of Rupert Murdoch? Why and how is it possible that newspapers are used to support a particular party or policy line? By what right do those with money appear to have so much influence over the fate of political parties, and why do politicians tolerate this state of affairs? Why is it acceptable for journalists to promise ministers favourable coverage on a certain issue in return for exclusive access to information on that issue? Is it proper that a large business such as Tescos is able to use its contacts and financial wherewithal to ensure that the planning system's rules are interpreted - or even altered through due process - to suit its interests? Is it proper that food supplies should be so strongly dominated by so few stores, that healthier foods should be the more expensive, and that the poor should suffer the worst diets?

Could we then go on to suggest that these features are merely symptoms of broader and deeper corruption within British society? Its political institutions have become career structures. The vast majority of schools and universities are now being transformed into workshops or 'skills' factories whose primary function is to churn out a labourforce with specific training in tasks favoured by businesses who have lobbied government the hardest. The justification for this narrowing of education is the need to finance welfare (especially health) in a highly competitive globalised world. In these factories, thought is necessarily fragmented, specialisms and qualifications multiply, and instruction in correct thought and practice has become the order of the day. In this disjointed world, held together by orthopraxy, a desire for things offers only the meanest release. Some of its citizens will do well financially through sport, music, entertainment, or hard-and-fast business. But outside their long working hours, the vast majority of the population have little release from their unfree existence save bouts of drunkenness, T.V., DIY, the intrigues of celebrities, and occasional excursions to nightclubs in Europe. Meanwhile, what are held to be the best, and extremely costly, private schools and universities (where a combination of increasing fees and still more costly living expenses will bar entry to all save those who are financially comfortable) are becoming instruments of power rather than centres of education. Their main function is to define the standards for intellectual excellence by which they are to measure themselves; to generate, or to inflate, certain questions into problems of national or global magnitude in order to attract funding; to satisfy the immediate interests and demands businesses (including their own); and to provide opportunities for their students to forge with each other relationships which, after graduation, will be invaluable to them professionally.

Why, then, should inheritance laws not be changed in favour of the wealthy? What better way of bolstering this educational and professional frame for a self-sustaining and exclusive elite? Who will care that the barriers to social mobility have once again have been raised and strengthened? The population is being transformed into an inarticulate mass which has little interest in voicing coherent critiques and is mostly unable to do so. Cowed by correct practice and platitudes, by the huge cathedrals to health which tower over them (symbols of their politicians' right to shape the world), and by fear of subversives from within and from without their own society, most people seem willing to accept the state's determination to increase its powers and surveillance over every aspect of its citizens' lives even to the extent that they must adhere to state-defined or state-licensed orthopraxy if they are to avoid prosecution.

We could argue, then, that the formalistion of the UK's political economy has served to legitimise corruption and to concentrate power, wealth, and influence in very few hands. Formalism has itself been turned into a shibboleth of propriety. The definitions of corruption which we outlined above - and the quality of fomalism which lie at their root - are, therefore, far from being 'value-neutral': they are cultural products of the West. To refuse to acknowledge this, and to insist that only the particular state of affairs which pertains in the UK and elsewhere in the developed 'west' is proper, blinds us to our own faults and robs us of an appreciation of the strengths and beauty of other ways. Such denials also condition us to the conviction that where reciprocity and hostility to profit dominate, where social, political, economic, public and private spheres of activity are blurred, and where status, responsibility, rights and ambitions are determined by ascription, corruption is bound to reach into every corner of life.

Nye definition critique

Nevertheless, the question, or problem, of relativity has long been recognised. Nye (*op.cit*) acknowledges that his public-office-centred definition is not entirely satisfactory in handling 'relativity standards'. And defence of these kinds of definitions is in many ways robust. First, there is nothing peculiarly 'western' about formalised behaviour, nor is it a quality particular to the modern age. Secondly, behaviour generally considered to be corrupt according to western standards is at least partially relevant in non-western and developing countries These countries have, rightly or wrongly, adopted, or have had imposed on them, western or western-style institutions, procedures, processes and conventions. Thirdly, if we accept that 'good', 'bad', 'proper', and 'improper' are relative qualities, then comparative analyses of corruption across different cultures *critical eval* becomes impossible. Relativity also hands to those in other societies with power and wealth a deal of license to justify any action they may wish to take. Moreover, if we accept relativity across different cultures, then are we not bound to accept relativity within any particular society? In which case, since public opinion is not uniform, who determines the standards of propriety? Are we now compelled to accept a lack of cohesion? Or do we accept that these standards may be determined by, say, one religious sect or linguistic group at the expense of another? We can take this line of questioning even further. If we accept relativity, then should we not also be prepared to accept individual relativity? Within a group that we might like to define by its culture, there may be differences. 'My' intentions as well as 'my' standards, beliefs, values, behaviour will not always be 'yours'. The fact that academics within the UK or the USA have different views over fundamental issues such as universalism, relativity, or the significance of individual and society, makes this point. If we are *not* prepared to accept individual relativity when we have already accepted cultural relativity, then we must explain why this is so. Is it enough the claim, for instance, that individuals do not have a sense of their individuality (or that any such sense is delusional) and that they are merely vehicles for culture or 'entanglement'?

Philp (1997), who focuses on political corruption, attempts to deal with the question of the relativity (or universality) of the proper state in the following way. Political relationships, he argues, comprise the hierarchical ordering of authority. That authority rests ultimately on the willingness of the citizen to concede the right to rule, usually on the basis of an appeal to principle such as consent, public utility, welfare or the common good; and this implies public standards of justification. These political relationships are similar to, but are not the same as, communal, patron-client, and market relationships. Political rule – of which there are many forms – only exists if political relationships are able to withstand competition from these other kinds of relationships. When these other kinds begin to inveigle political relationships, corruption may be indicated. The presence of corruption, however, is not determined by the fact or extent of encroachment, nor by success or failure in maintaining political rule. Behaviour (such as nepotism and patron-clientelism) and its effects (such as the weakening or crumbling of state institutions), only amount to corruption when those who are behaving in these ways had open to them the choice to act differently. The presence and extent of corruption, then, is measured by counterfactuals[*] – by what could have been done otherwise and, given the wider social and economic context, would have been more effective. It does not take much imagination, argues Philp (p.451), to recognize

> 'that the political norms for the conduct of office can become inoperable under certain socio-economic conditions. The kinds of benefits generated by a political system – security, the rule of law, citizenship, and so on – are not easily quantified or weighed against other types of goods, and they are invariably long-term in character....When these benefits are threatened by political chaos, or social or economic disruption, there comes a point at

---

[*] Arguably the term is used more properly to describe regularities inferred from a law: if I were to do x, then y would happen.

which it is irrational not to seek other gains or more partial, less general forms of political goods – for example, by seeking profit that can be turned into hard currency, by building a following (or seeking a patron) so as to provide some of the benefits of a stable political system albeit in a less general form, or by falling back on kinship or other types of communal relations for the delivery of goods and services.'

The idea that these activities are corrupt - the thought that people could act in some other (and moral) way if only they possessed a degree of saintliness and heroism - must be discounted as a counterfactual.

The polity, then, may crumble as it is subverted and strangled by communal, patron-client or market relations, and the state may fall apart, without a condition of corruption ever having established itself. Indeed, it is possible, argues Philp, to assert categorically that states are not corrupt unless, counterfactually, they could be other than they are, 'were it not for the way that political norms and rules are being ignored or bent by a faction, group, or individual to maintain their dominance and secure their interests over and against the political and broader cultural norms of the community' (p. 452).

For Philp, corruption is defined by the presence of opportunities to behave differently and more effectively. It is with this provision that political corruption may be understood as the decay of the natural, proper order of political rule. A more precise definition, therefore, depends merely upon the 'take' of the natural order.

But what are we to make of these arguments? The view that corruption is a deviation from what is held as proper is not difficult to accept. Much of the rest of the discussion, however, seems designed primarily to steer an intricate course between what Philp (and many other writers) regard as two equally repugnant options: stipulative definitions of corruption following western norms (commonly thought to be universal by those who adhere to them); and the cultural relativist's appeal to local norms and standards (pp. 441-2). One question which immediately arises is this: does the repugnance felt towards these options reflect universal or relative norms and standards? Moreover, if norms are so strong and shape our thoughts and lives so profoundly, then how is it that the western academic (or some western academics) are able to stand outside the boundaries of their influence, and from there observe and appreciate them dispassionately?

Further questions arise when that explicit declaration of repugnance with cultural relativism is placed alongside Philp's concern that the kind of relativism in which we indulge ourselves is not simply moral relativism:

> 'that might seem like a price worth paying to avoid western stipulation. But the danger of this move is that the damage to one's analysis spreads beyond moral relativism to a conceptual relativism' (p.442).

And this makes comparison across different cultures impossible. The license which relativism gives to actions and behaviour may be preferable to that permitted by universalism, but conceptual relativism takes us beyond the pale.

Are we to conclude that intellectual convenience (in the conduct of cross-cultural analysis) takes precedence over the license which relativity and universalism give to actions and behaviour on the street? If so, and if, by implication,* we are prepared to admit and accommodate a degree of moral relativism as well universalism, then should we not ask whether concerns with conceptual relativism - and the subsequent determination to identify commonalities (such as political, market, patron-client and communal relationships) - are expressions of occidental insularity and arrogance? It begins to seem as if the notion of counterfactuals is being used to balance intellectual expedience with the ethical mores of some quarters of the scholarly community.

---

* Philps' unspoken assumption that academic concepts are free of moral judgements is highly questionable

Intention and consequences

(ii) The argument pursued by Philp also provides us with an illustration of another reason why it is so difficult to pin down a precise definition and understanding of corruption: the uncertainty over whether or not we can, or should, separate intention from consequences. Is an act corrupt if it has no consequences, or no consequences of any significance? Is an act corrupt if it was performed without the intention either of distorting formal rules and procedures, or of serving a personal agenda? Philp is clearly of the view that we can and should separate intention from consequence. Even though we may act in ways that will bring misery, chaos, and destruction, it is quite possible, if we follow his argument, to absolve oneself of the charge of corruption. If we can make the case that we were compelled by circumstances to act as we did and that we could not have acted otherwise, then our actions cannot be described as corrupt: intention is everything.

Yet there are problems with this position. How are we to judge intention? How do you distinguish between my genuine *belief* that I had no choice but to behave as I did, and my *claim* that I had no choice? And if you judge me only by what *you* say my intention was, irrespective of my action and its consequences, then how can I defend myself against any accusation that you might wish to make? If, on the other hand, we are concerned only with consequences, and not with intentions, then are we to regard as corrupt every poor decision, every poorly executed plan, every departure from correct practice, every incident of incompetence, and every mistake?

Morality and law

(iii) The doubts surrounding the 'fit' between morality, the law, and corruption also make it difficult to reach a clear and generally recognised definition of corruption. We cannot necessarily equate morality with propriety, nor immorality with corruption. Nor does a contravention or observance of laws equate with corruption, propriety, morality or immorality. It is quite possible to break a law

18

without being corrupt, and to act corruptly by observing that same law. For instance, it might be thought that a failure to legislate against hunting foxes with dogs and against smoking in enclosed public areas was corrupt - partly because it reflected the influence of class and business interests within the British parliament - as well as immoral. Yet we can also argue that the introduction of such legislation was little more than an arbitrary and intolerant act of prejudice, and one which sets a dangerous precedent. There are many things which any one of us finds distasteful or immoral or even corrupt but against which we do not legislate. And many of these things - if measured by the intensity and length of pain experienced, or by the sheer numbers of people (rather than animals) who suffer - inflict a much greater cruelty and a far heavier burden on public finances: producing diesel exhaust, driving cars, flying airliners, manufacturing arms and fast-foods, eating too much, drinking too heavily, and being bad parents. To have failed until recently to legislate against hunting and smoking was neither immoral nor corrupt. To the contrary it was (in its preservation of tolerance) moral and just. From this point of view, whilst hunting with dogs and smoking in enclosed public areas are now illegal, it is neither corrupt nor immoral to flout that legislation.

Gradation

(iv) A fourth reason why it is so difficult to reach a clear and generally recognised definition of corruption – and it is one that is closely tied to the question of relativity – is the uncertainty surrounding the point at which the proper state is no longer proper (or indeed, moral and lawful) and becomes corrupt (or indeed immoral or unlawful). We can phrase the problem another way: at what point are we no longer prepared to accept that the quality of an act is in doubt because it may be viewed from many different perspectives?

3.0 Extent and measurement

Given these problems of definition there must be doubts about our measurement of corruption: what precisely *is* being measured? The problem is compounded by the strong likelihood that many acts of corruption are hidden, and by the use of allegation and counter-allegation as weapons in political battles for power and influence. Just how possible is it, then, to gain a reasonably accurate sense of the extent and depth of corruption?

Governments and their agencies, as well as NGOs and private organisations (such as Business Risk Analysis), produce various estimates of levels of corruption in many countries. Some measure the number of corrupt acts reported or prosecuted; but most take the form of indexes which measure not the number of corrupt acts but perceptions of the extent of corruption. These perceptions are gleaned either from panels of experts or from residents or from both. In the light of these indexes, and with historical accounts of corruption in mind, it is probably fair to say that corruption has been, and continues to be, found in all societies and at all times. Modern indexes also appear to show that corruption is more widespread and more entrenched (or at least this is perceived to be so) in countries which are either less developed or in the midst of transformation from a communist state to a market economy. This observation has tended to lead to the suspicion or, in the minds of some, to the certainty that there exists an inverse relation between levels of economic development and corruption: stronger and wealthier economies are less corrupt than poorer and weaker ones. These measures are important for those of us who are interested in explaining and formulating measures to deal with corruption, in reconstructing states, and in directing investments.

> support with UK quote, pg-10

There are good reasons, and there is much incentive, to think that these estimates of the perceived level of corruption are reliable. First, the experts from whom views are solicited are chosen precisely because they have an intimate knowledge of a country's business, political and bureaucratic communities and their workings. Secondly, sampling, survey and statistical techniques of various kinds are applied to reduce the possible bias within a polling organisation and in its analyses. Thirdly, the ratings (the final indexes) are similar for each country even though different organisations use different techniques; nor do these ratings vary much from year to year; and if rating do rise or fall for a particular country over time, very similar movements are recorded by the different organisations. Cross-national rates, Treisman (2000, p.400) believes, are 'highly correlated with each other and highly correlated over time'. Fourthly, the results of surveys of experts are matched by the results of surveys of ordinary residents. Fifthly, the indexes which are produced for profit continue to find a ready market. This suggests that they are, on the whole, unbiased and reliable. Sixthly, these indexes are all that we have to work with.

There are, however, a number of problems which, it might be argued, cannot be ignored or pushed to the back of one's mind. To begin with, the point is often made (and it is, for reasons that we will come to later, a very significant point) that whilst perceptions are subjective, they influence behaviour including, in particular, investments. Indexes which measure subjective perceptions of corruption are therefore important and valuable. All this we may well be prepared to accept. But if we are measuring the perception of corruption, then why do we so often go on to explain the causes and effects of corruption itself rather than changes in our perceptions of corruption? This is a rather different kind of study.

Second, if we accept that these perceptions influence subsequent thought and actions, then we must accept that experts and residents may be swayed by, for instance, a country's economic performance. If they are of the view that there is an inverse relationship between that performance and corruption, then a strong economy may lead them to the view that there must be little corruption. By the same token, a badly performing economy may lead them to interpret all problems or inefficiencies as symptoms of corruption. Perceptions may be influenced similarly by highly publicised scandals, or by the allegations which politicians throw at each other, or by the absence of such publicity and allegations.

A third, and similar, point is that the ideological agenda of an organisation may have a bearing upon the indexes that it produces. An organisation whose members have, say, a strong belief in the moral and practical value of the free market may be more likely to view degrees of government intervention as corrupt or grey activities; and this may influence either the questions asked, or their phrasing, or the interpretation of responses.

Fourthly, it may suit experts - especially if they are connected with political, bureaucratic and business communities - to be more critical of a government which is, in their view, either unwilling and unable to stimulate economic growth, or does not favour the expert's own interests. Meanwhile, a government which is, in the expert's view, doing what the expert thinks should be done, may be presented in a more flattering light.

What all this suggests is that we must treat with caution our assessments of the extent and nature of corruption within a country. We are not always in agreement over our definitions of corruption; and there exist complex interactions among those who analyse and interpret corruption, those who participate in its measurement, and the practice and views of bureaucrats, politicians and businesses. Distinguishing between practice, analysis and interpretation is no easy thing. The mutual influences exerted among the measurement of perception, the perception itself, the people who measure, and the people whose perceptions are being measured, are such that our perception indexes are probably best used to craft representations of a particular country. We must keep in mind the possibility that our estimates of corruption do no more than strengthen the beliefs which we already hold about any particular society, and may thereby serve only to further undermine or bolster confidence or cynicism in that society.

4.0 Effects

Much of the interest in, and concern with, the effects of corruption is directed at the condition of the economy and public services and, in connexion with these activities, at the efficacy of government and bureaucracy. These discussions are closely bound up with our understandings of the causes of corruption and with our definitions of what we believe a proper state to be. Since our definitions and understandings of these causes are manifold, it is not surprising that what are held to be corruption's effects – or what are sometimes called its functions - are extensive, and that our interpretations of those effects alter with our sense of the proper state. When corruption is thought to reflect a struggle to preserve the non-western, then it may be viewed more favourably. Those who feel that market democracies are intrinsically flawed, who see there only structures of power and exploitation, may also sympathise with 'corruption'. The conception of a proper state as a reasonably stable market economy set within a democratic polity also strongly colours much of the commentary on the positive, as well as the negative, effects of corruption.

4.1 Corruption's negative effects

If one holds that the general well being of society is rooted in each individual's pursuit of profit, then corruption is antipathetic to that ideal. It is compatible neither with fair opportunity, nor with fair competition, nor with competent and light government. Corrupt merchants work not only in their own interests, but against the interests of others. Energies within government and its bureaucracy are quickly consumed by the politicians', bureaucrats', and merchants' struggle to secure, maintain and defend personal advantage, such that any vision they may have had for government, and for the governed, soon dissolves. A number of more specific and malign effects are often identified.[*]

---

[*] The discussion is drawn in particular from: Bayley, 1966; Nye, 1967; Huntington, 1970; McMullan, 1961; Leff, 1964; Myrdal, 1968; Bhargava and Bolongaita, 2004.

MARKET IMPERFECTIONS

First, corruption deepens or creates market imperfections. By extracting direct payments, and by compelling merchants to spend a good deal of their time (and a deal of their money) setting up and working networks of officials and politicians, corruption increases costs to businesses in much the same way as an arbitrary tax. Corruption also favours the larger and well-connected businesses, encourages rent-seeking behaviour and, by distorting incentives, misdirects the merchant's energy and talent. For all these reasons, and perhaps most damagingly, corruption discourages foreign investment.

UNDERMINING GOVT. CONTROL

Secondly, corruption works against national consolidation. It does so partly by undermining government control: authority cannot be effectively delegated; the efficiency of government and other agencies is weakened; meritocracies are destroyed or prevented from emerging; faith in public services is eroded; and politicians, bureaucrats, and citizens are encouraged to treat each other with suspicion and cynicism. And now that it is believed, rightly or wrongly, that corruption is endemic, there is little incentive or reason to remain uncorrupted oneself. As distrust *within* government (and *in* government) deepens, and as politicians form cliques around social kernels (such as ethnicity, kinship, friendship, language, educational and professional background, religion, or place of origin), factions throughout society multiply, producing intense cleavages that may lead to violent conflict.

Thirdly, corruption distorts government priorities, policies, and planning. While corruption raises the costs to business, it reduces public revenues and, at the same time, increases the burden of government procurements. For example, it is *E.g.* estimated that in Thailand and Indonesia procurement costs are somewhere between 20% and 100% higher than they would otherwise have been (Nakata, 1978; Gray, 1979; Wade, 1982; Business Week 1993). Corruption may also shift public expenditure towards those items (such as defence) that will attract larger and more easily concealed bribes, and away from those items (such as education) that will not (Mauro, 1998). Direction is also lost as bureaucrats either slow up, or create more labyrinthine, processes in order to attract 'speed' money. Misdirection of public finances may damage not just the occasional project or sector, but an entire political economy. In the Philippines, for example, it is estimated that from the late 1970s until the late 1990s, $48 billion were misappropriated, surpassing the country's entire foreign debt (Reuters Newswire, 1997). The diversion of aid donations may take place on a similar scale. As much as $30 billion of aid to Africa has ended up in the foreign bank accounts of African leaders. This amounts to twice the annual GDP of Ghana, Kenya and Uganda combined (Pedersen, 1996).

It is worth pointing out that the impacts of these costs, direct and indirect, on development are not uniform (Asian Development Bank, 1998, p.17). Some countries seem better able to tolerate corruption than others. The degree of tolerance is said to depend upon a number of conditions. One is the form in which corruption is practiced. In some countries, corruption is well organised, payoffs are known in advance, and they are concentrated at the highest levels. Leading politicians will take their cut and then ensure that firms and businesses do not meet with additional demands nor suffer interference from local politicians and bureaucrats. Another condition is the manner in which the money taken through these payoffs is spent. Is it spent on a luxury lifestyle overseas, or is it put into industries and productive activity at home?

But although a level of corruption can be tolerated in some countries, many commentators would argue that countries with higher levels of corruption are unlikely to perform as well economically as they would have done otherwise. One IMF study appears to demonstrate that a one-point improvement in the corruption index translates into increases of 2.9% of GDP in the investment rate and 1.3% in the annual per capita rate of GDP growth (Mauro, 1995). The World Bank, too, found that counties with lower levels of corruption attract significantly more investment (World Bank, 1997; Wei, 1997).

4.2 Corruption's positive effects

It is, however, also commonly argued that corruption may take on many positive aspects* especially, though not exclusively, when it is thought to be a consequence of the market shaking itself free of illiberal, inefficient, unnecessary, and uneconomical government.

(i) It is often argued that corruption works as a corrective to those governments and bureaucracies whose prime concerns are to enhance their own control over the rest of society, and to preserve the established symbols of power and status. Such governments are, consequently, either indifferent to entrepreneurs and the requirements of a thriving economy, or hostile to merchants who are, in any case, often social and political outsiders – a position commonly emphasised by their ethnicity. This friction between those motivations and interests which are political, and those which are largely economic, is often understood to be a feature of societies in the midst of a transition from a condition of traditionalism to one of modernity. It is, therefore, a problem which, for many writers, is characteristic of, but not restricted to, developing countries today. Tensions between merchants and politicians (and their bureaucracy) were a feature of ancient civilizations, and remain a feature of today's modern states. We need only to remember: the ambiguous status of merchants throughout the history of Imperial China; or the antipathy of government and unions towards profit and business in the UK during the 1960s and 1970s; or the tensions between state and merchants which found expression in socialist China through the conservatives (who were tolerant of limited private trade) and the Maoist radicals (who did their best to eradicate trade

---

* The discussion is drawn in particular from: Bayley, 1966; Nye, 1967; Huntington, 1970; McMullan, 1961; Leff, 1964; Klitgaard, 1991.

from a society that was held to be both Chinese and thoroughly modern).* In these kinds of circumstances - where government and its bureaucracy intervenes heavily in economic affairs, and businesses find it difficult if not impossible to operate without official consent - corruption becomes the *sine qua non* of any firm if it is to survive as a going concern. Through the corruption of officials, firms produce oases in which they are insulated from unpredictable political intervention. Here they have the space and time to experiment, innovate, and invest; to build up markets and revenues; and to establish themselves gradually as effective political operators. As their networks expand, corruption begins to compel government to make better choices. This effect is worked not just occasionally but systematically, such that government policy is first deformed and then braided into sub-streams which may prove advantageous for entrepreneurs, officials, and the country as a whole. And as government begins to lighten its hand, corruption begins to intensify as firms pursue limited opportunities with greater vigour, increasing the pressure upon government to quicken the pace of liberalisation still further.

Corruption, then, may bring a degree of economic commonsense to the polity: it may undermine a systematic bias against both the market (a bias often driven by ideology) and private income; and it provides capital which, if invested productively rather than salted away into bank accounts overseas, may help to stimulate development (Nye, *op.cit.;* Khan, *op. cit.*). Corruption may also imitate market efficiencies. For instance, the speed money which merchants pay to public officials shortens not only the time they wait, but also the overall length of the queue; those companies which can afford to pay large bribes are those which are already efficient enough to bid for tenders at the lowest cost; and if bribes are centralised and effectively monitored, a system is produced which is more effective and less costly (to the briber) than one in which different ministries, agencies and levels of local government all set their own levies independently. Still more efficient, or so it is sometimes argued, is a system in which a firm need

---

* See, in particular, Solinger, 1984.

pay only a single, large bribe. This may take many forms, including contributions to a party's campaign slush-fund.

(ii) A second positive effect, or function, of corruption is to improve the quality of personnel brought into political office and into the civil service. By offering a way to supplement poor wages, able men and women (who might have been attracted to other professions) are encouraged to enter public service. Capable people may also be drawn into public office through other, non-financial, forms of corruption. It is quite possible, argues Bayley (*op. cit.*), that a group successful in penetrating the civil service through nepotism has, for this very reason, the qualities necessary for making decisions and implementing policies effectively.

(iii) A third effect of corruption is to stabilize the polity. A bureaucracy whose ranks are swollen - whether through nepotism, or through the perceived opportunities for illicit money-making which membership is thought to offer - is unlikely to have become more efficient. But it does keep large number of young and comparatively well-educated and ambitious people off the streets, and it gives them a stake in 'the system'. And by accommodating something of the widespread expectation that officials should meet their obligations to their own extended families, the number of people with an interest in maintaining that system is multiplied many times over. For those outside the system, too, corruption may provide a tangible and personal means of influencing the polity at many levels, from its legislature and highest-ranking executives, down to the everyday gritty bureaucratic routine on the ground. Corruption, then, works to make government more human, reducing frustration with formal (and often ineffectual) institutions and procedures. Concomitants of this humanising effect may include a softening of the perceptions which rulers, officials, and citizens may have of each other, and some redistribution of wealth and influence from those with much to those with little.

A society's sharpening focus on financial and material wealth may also, as Bayley (*op. cit.*) puts it, act as a solvent for matters over which compromise would otherwise be impossible. With corruption, a common point of interest is introduced, bridging divisions along caste, tribe, ethnicity, language, kinship, ideology and religion. These networks of corrupt exchanges may help to integrate elites with ordinary citizens, and to overcome discrimination against minority groups. Such connexions may also help to lessen tensions between, say, civil servants (who may be impatient with, and contemptuous of, the populist and transitory whims of politicians) and politicians (who see civil servants as cold, insensitive and rigid technocrats); or between those groups with political control and those with financial power. Corruption, then, through its quality of self-interest, may bind together groups that would otherwise think of themselves as different and divided. And, in doing so, corruption may even take on the shape of formal institutions. For example, payments or donations made by firms to political parties in order to procure influence, may also help to strengthen parties. Without such funding, parties might either be swayed by foreign interests or fall into decay, indiscipline, factionalism, and disunity, and take the entire country with them.

In these ways - by helping the market to work, by improving the quality of personnel, and by reducing tensions, inequalities and divisions - corruption also works as a 'functional equivalence' for violence. Historical precedence for this can be found in the developed world, or so it is often suggested. This line of thought is sometimes taken even further with the suggestion that just as western civilization's entrepreneurial class emerged from the sale of monopoly rights and private access public resources, so corruption in the developing world today both reflects and facilitates market transition. Khan (*op. cit.*), who makes a very similar argument, begins by noting that the economic effects of corruption are two-fold. The first is the cost of bribe itself: has that money been diverted away from productive investment? or has it been spent at home or overseas? The second is the economic consequence of the new rights (or the re-allocation of rights) that have been secured through bribes. Whether the effects of corruption hinder or promote growth depends upon the structure of patron-client relations. It is these structures that explain why some countries perform badly and why some, despite corruption, are able to generate high rates of economic growth. If bribes are organised such that they allow a flexible re-allocation of rights and do not interfere with economic rationality, then corruption will encourage growth. For example, in the Indian subcontinent corruption has tended to work against growth because a strong non-capitalist class has been locked into patron-client networks with politicians, bureaucrats and capitalists. This made the re-allocation of rights and resources difficult. By contrast, the structure of patron-client relationships (and so the effects of corruption on growth) in many parts of East and Southeast Asia has been rather different. In South Korea the concentration of power in the hands of central politicians and bureaucrats has meant that they have had no need to worry about an intermediate (or non-capitalist) class in Korean society. In return for substantial payments, bureaucrats and politicians allocated rights to capitalists in ways that maximised long-run growth. In Malaysia, a strong intermediate Malay class held political and bureaucratic power, while economic power was concentrated largely in the hands of a Chinese minority. The politicians took pay-offs, but these were centralised; and in this, and in other ways, payments were organised such that, on the whole, there was little interference with the economically rational decisions of Chinese entrepreneurs. In Thailand the political elite was populated by capitalists with whom Chinese entrepreneurs were seamlessly integrated. This elite also took over local political networks, removing Thailand's intermediate (non-capitalist) class and leaving itself free to reallocate rights among its own factions. This process of factional re-allocation was highly competitive, but for this reason permitted flexible responses to the changing requirements of economic growth.

It is important to say that the positive effects, or functions, of corruption detailed in these kinds of arguments are not thought to be applicable at all times to all

30

*Eval.

societies or to all parts of one society. It is often emphasised that the nature of corruption's effects – whether positive or negative, or functional or dysfunctional – depends upon the kind of corruption and the circumstances. For instance, top-heavy corruption (corruption in the upper echelons of society) may be de-stabilising especially if entry routes for younger and ambitious men and women into those corrupt networks are blocked. Taken together, however, these arguments do lead us to an interesting conclusion. If the kinds of advantages which corruption is said to bring to a society are not uncommon, then could it not be argued that corruption is as much the *consequence*, as it is a *cause*, of poor government? Corruption, in other words, may be a spontaneous, commonsensical, and reasoned way of dealing with problems - such as slow economic growth, economic decline, incompetent personnel, tension, instability, and violence - that a government has failed to deal with. We might further argue that such problems are made worse by governments who - anxious to compensate for their ineffectiveness and to prove their modern credentials - first blame corrupt elements, and then draft too many laws and procedures, set out too many standards for behaviour, and attempt to observe all of these too closely.

There are, it must also be said, counter-arguments to these more positive views of corruption. And it is interesting to note that some of these doubts expressed by Brooks (1910) pre-empt the more favourable interpretations outlined above by more than fifty years.

(i) The suggestion that a 'wide-open' - or, in other words, a less regulated and more corrupt – country has a more effective and vibrant economy ignores the fact that, whilst some people do gain as a result of corruption, many other people suffer. Social scientists today make a very similar point: the systematic impacts of corruption are not considered. Although particular instances of corruption may indeed have benefits, those instances, when taken together, work to degrade the system as a whole (Asian Development Bank, *op. cit.*). Those who engage in

Critical

Counter to positive effect.

Critical

corruption see the world only through their own limited and selfish perspective. Many of the apparent benefits of corruption (such as enhancing civil servants' income or making government more efficient), only appear to be beneficial when set against a public sector that is performing badly and inefficiently. And a specific instance of corruption seems to mark an improvement only when viewed against the backdrop of the wider problems for which corruption is itself responsible. The greater good comes from cleaning up the public sector. Moreover, whilst it is not easy to show that in all instances corruption is detrimental to economic growth, this does not mean we can reject the general statement that, in most countries and most times, corruption works against or slows down economic progress. Instances of beneficial corruption are not incompatible with the empirical evidence of the general association between low levels of development and high levels of corruption.

(ii) Secondly, a disregard for specific laws, conventions, and regulations, may develop into a disregard for laws, conventions, and regulations in general. Again, social scientists today make a very similar point: corruption is not discriminatory. Once officials and citizens begin to ignore bad laws and bad systems, they may also start to avoid good ones. A customs official bribed to expedite shipments of medical equipment for a hospital might also be willing to give the nod to drug smugglers (*ibid.*).

(iii) The argument that corrupt officials and merchants are not necessarily incompetent or unpatriotic, or that corruption is merely a foible which sometimes accompanies great abilities, is also viewed with a deal of scepticism. That weakness attends strengths, and that we should be tolerant of ourselves, is a very sound point. But why must the able practice corruption to garner wealth and power? And at what point does tolerance become license?

(iv) Suggestions that corruption is a functional equivalence for violence, that it brings cohesion and stability, and that it saves us from mob rule, depend, in Brooks' view, on an unjust portrayal of ordinary people, most of whom want only an opportunity to make an honest living. We might add that whilst corruption networks may reach across existing divides and open up opportunities for some people, they may also create new divisions and close down opportunities for other people. If old networks die and new ones are created quickly enough, then perhaps a kind of social mobility and political stability can be maintained. But is this kind of arrangement likely to prove stable and reliable over the longer term?

(v) Finally, in response to the suggestion that corruption is merely an expression of an evolutionary process, Brooks us to show that the benefits of this evolution are greater than its costs. Or are we suggesting that evolution is merely an a-moral statement of fact? If so, then have we not provided a rational justification for any amount of evil? As for suggestions that corruption is a response to ineffective government or a viable excuse for political and administrative ineptitude, we could respond with very a similar question: are we not merely rationalising self-centred behaviour?

5.0 Conclusions

It would seem that we have not come very far in our attempt to define corruption and gain a sense of its extent and depth. This is not surprising: the ability to set out with any certainty and precision what we mean by corruption presumes that we have in our possession a fairly sound and commonly agreed understanding of corruption's causes and effects; and this, as we shall see, we do not yet have within our grasp. We can, perhaps, bring a little more clarity to our meaning of corruption only after we have reviewed its various explanations. However, two related questions arise from our discussion so far, both of which might bear further consideration.

(i) First, could it be that corruption appears to be so prevalent (it is, we have said, to be found in all countries and at all times) precisely because we are unsure about its meaning, or, perhaps more accurately, because to each of us it means many different things? Corruption, then, is not a specific phenomenon. It is an interpretation made of movements, changes and apparent differences in practice, perception and values. Whilst we were, a little earlier in this chapter, somewhat critical of Philp's argument, the general thrust of his paper is important: it illustrates a shift in emphasis away from a very specific and technical examination of corruption ('the phenomenon'), and towards an attempt to understand the broad social context and the changes therein.

(ii) A second question, therefore, is whether the way in which social scientists think about corruption fits with its practice? Is our thought too awkward and segmented to deal with the multiple aspects of the social world? The very categories with which we describe corruption and its causes and effects - as well as our spheres of activity (such as economic, social, political, and bureaucratic) and our institutions and practices - reflect the highly formalised thought and practice of the social scientist. We are, in other words, applying modes of thought which are incompatible with the behaviour and thought we are trying to understand. Consequently, our heavily defined categories of corruption seem to fit only occasionally (and only for a moment) the whirling dimensional complexity of the street.

CHAPTER 2
The Causes of Corruption:
structure and culture

1.0 Introduction

We turn now to consider how we might account for the presence of corruption. What are its causes? A large number of explanations have been proposed over the last fifty years or so, and these may be thought to comprise three broad categories: the institutional (or structural); the cultural (or anthropological); and the moral. There exists between the first two a dialogue that is, we argue here, of some importance to an understanding of how we study corruption. The third category is less popular in today's literature. Nevertheless, it is one that we will consider in chapter 4, for its value may have been underestimated.

2.0 Structural explanations

If measured by the sheer quantity of literature it generates, the institutional - or structural - perspective is by far the most influential. Corruption is explained: either by reference to the arrangements of rules, procedures, roles and patterns of behaviour within specific spheres of activity (say economic, social, political and bureaucratic); or by reference to the historical evolution of the present institutional and behavioural patterns that cross an entire society or large swathes of its different spheres; or by some combination of the two – the narrow and the expansive.

2.1 Economics and politics

For many observers – and especially, as Bardhan (1997) points out, for liberal economists – the single most important cause of corruption is the state's heavy regulation of its people and their livelihoods. Corruption is, in other words, a consequence of the panoply of licenses, permits, rules, and procedures which, intentionally or not, contravene or ignore natural economic behaviour and survival.

A similar view is taken by Rose-Ackerman (1999) whose study begins with the assumption that 'self-interest, including an interest in the well-being of one's family and peer group' (p.2) is a universal human motivator. It is managed best in 'the archetypal competitive market where self-interest is transmuted into productive activities that lead to efficient resource use', and worst 'through war – a destructive struggle over wealth that ends up destroying the resource base that motivated the fight in the first place. In between are situations where people use resources both for productive purposes and to gain an advantage in dividing up the benefits of economic activity – called "rent-seeking" by economists' (p.2).

An example of this middle way is to be found in the Philippines. Drawing on a number of writers, including Crouch, (1979, 1985), Evans, (1989, 1992) and Weber (1968, 1981), Hutchcroft provides a broad historical and structural explanation for patron-client relationships and for the more generally personalistic quality of the Philippines' political economy. The Spanish failure to engage in state building provided room both for the emergence of strong British, American, and Chinese trading houses, and for the entrenchment of a Chinese-mestizo landed élite. This decentralisation of power was reinforced by the Philippines' American rulers, who concerned themselves mainly with the construction of representative institutions, while leaving outside those institutions oligarchs with their own strong economic and social bases. After independence, these oligarchs - either directly or through their proxies - moved in and out of those institutions at will, and, as they did so, continued to maintain and build up their own external social and economic power bases. Any disquiet which may have been felt in the United States was easily salved by opening up the archipelago's military facilities to the Americans. Meanwhile, in the provinces, local patrons drew money, materials, and authority, towards themselves through their personal relationships with the centre. Family businesses, faced with hostile and unpredictable circumstances, established complex and aggressive networks of relationships through which they could influence the political economy to their own advantage and to the disadvantage of their enemies and competitors. Thanks in part to this competition, and in part to public education and examinations, the membership of the elite proved to be socially mobile. But the centre remained weak, and the state was left vulnerable to influence from powerful individuals and factionalised groups operating outside its institutions. Thus was the Philippines exposed to exploitation by competing oligarchies and cronies (*ibid.*).

For Rose-Ackerman (*op. cit.*), then, an understanding the causes of corruption requires an understanding of the ways in which self-interest is mismanaged. These take a number of forms, most of which are largely structural in nature. The first is described by public programmes, especially those which serve no legitimate public good. These create bottlenecks and constraints, and give too much discretion to officials. The second is described by bureaucracies based on patronage and political loyalty. These characteristics are likely to be intimately associated with low salaries, the presence of conflicts of interests, inadequate systems of rewards and punishment, over-staffing, and the bureaucracy's involvement in too many kinds of activities.

The third is described by the concentration of political power in too few hands. This is most obvious when an autocratic ruler faces weak private actors, or when large private companies face weak states from which they can extract high levels of benefits without paying large bribes. By diffusing power a democratic system provides incumbents with an incentive to be honest and citizens with avenues for complaint, and thereby helps to limit corruption. But democracy is no panacea. Power imbalances within a democracy - and the resulting incentives for corruption - often emerge from the complex interaction of structural features including, in particular, the electoral and legislative processes, methods of campaign funding and political cleavages. One such feature is geographically defined constituencies with concentrations of people who will benefit from government programmes. These programmes are easily transformed by politicians into favours which they might then distribute to narrowly focussed interests groups. Another feature is the availability, or unavailability, of these benefits to wealthy groups. Yet another comprises the extent of political instability (due either to competition or to ideological rivalry), and the extent to which this leads politicians to feel that they have only a short time to get as much out of the system for themselves as they can. The need to finance political campaigns; an electorate that expects personal and direct rewards from candidates in exchange for their votes; and the presence of conflicts of interest: these features, too, make it more likely that politicians and civil servants will use their positions to further their own business interests or those of their family and friends. This concern is particularly acute when salaries are low, and when there is little or no state funding for political campaigns. The absence of strong checks and balances among and within the different branches and institutions of government - such that authority begins to build up in the legislature, executive, or judiciary - may also encourage corruption. Under these circumstances, officials may, in return for rewards or in the face of threats, begin to peddle breaches in rules, procedures and process. This is still more likely: if government fails to provide either clear guidance on expected standards of behaviour or information on its expenditures, revenues, legislation, and the legislative process; when the judiciary is weakened by inexperience, low salaries, a heavy case load and an excessive bureaucracy; and when the activities of the media and NGOs are restricted.

While Rose-Ackerman emphasises economic self-interest, other writers emphasise the working out of political self-interest. After all, it would seem likely that in a poorly developed economy attempts will be made to transform material wealth or kinship and other ties into a measure of influence within government, while in an advanced economy the reverse will be true.

Scott (1969 b), for instance, argues that much – though not all – corrupt behaviour may be understood as a functional equivalent for political influence. The structural features of the polity merely affect the style and incidence of corruption. Where the formal channels for influence are restricted, corruption is likely to be more extensive. In Thailand, the formal positions of authority were not open to the country's largely Chinese business community who - if they were to safeguard and advance their own business interests - had to establish informal relationships with individual clique leaders in the Thai military and bureaucracy. These connexions were wholly illegal, but they profited both the Thai elite and Chinese businesses. By contrast, businesses in Japan, working collectively through associations, channeled funds into the coffers of the LDP which, in government, took their business interests into account. The Thai case, argues Scott, was corrupt; the Japanese case was not. In short, corruption emerges where - in the view of those who are seeking advantage - the regularised formal channels for securing political influence do not work or are not present.

Waterbury (1973) makes a very similar point, arguing that corruption is a

> 'variant of the broader phenomenon of patronage. Patronage is founded upon asymmetrical relation between a powerful person or group of persons and their clients who seek protection, favour and reward from the patrons. At the same time, to an important extent the patron is powerful as a result of the size and nature of his clientele, and is able to protect and reward his supporters

because he uses them to strengthen his hand in bargaining for scarce resources. A patron...need not be a public official; he can attract clientele on the basis of his wealth or his control of or access to scarce resources such as jobs, or land or arms. However, when a patron occupies a public position or extracts favours from those in public positions, patronage and corruption overlap' (p.537).

Patronage, then, is merely substitute for political influence, and outside formalised institutions it is an entirely legitimate practice. It only becomes corruption when it is taken into formal institutions and there begins to restrict the legitimate channels through which influence is exercised. In these circumstances patronage both constitutes corruption and, by distorting or blocking legitimate channels, may stimulate further corruption.

Theobald (1999), however, goes further and argues that the patronage, whether motivated by political or economic self-interest, does little more than describe the salient features of social organisation in the context of underdevelopment. It is not the existence of patronage that is important in an understanding of corruption, but the fact that, in the case of developing countries, profit and rent-seeking are concentrated on the limited area of the state. As a consequence of this pressure, demands for goods and services necessarily spill out through informal, personal channels. This contrasts with developed countries where demand is diffused through a variety of formal organisations and across many spheres of activity. Theobald cites the example of Chequita's contribution to the Democratic Party's funds the day after the US trade representative Kantor asked the WTO to raise its case against European tariffs. 'A key aspect of the transaction was that the route was suitably discreet; not to central party funds where it would have been recorded openly, but to state-level organisations. The main point is that although transacted through the structure of formal organisations, this series of exchanges was probably no less personal or covert than those embodied in what might be regarded as patron-client relations' (p.499).

If we accept that corruption is the practice of patronage in ways that are not yet formalised or legitimised, then could we perhaps argue that in the institutional quality of investment channels in mainland China we are seeing a formalisation of patronage and a decline in corruption (Hodder, 2006). A similar observation is made by Khan (1998). As new wealth-owning groups form they are unlikely to have secured agreement on the shape of legal framework for the allocation of rights to resources and wealth. Neither their rights to wealth nor the class as a whole is likely to be perceived as legitimate. 'To put it simply, the state is allocating rights and resources at a time when a new capitalist class is emerging. Given the long-run even inter-generational consequences of these allocations, there are huge incentives to dispute, contest and attempt to change all such allocations' (p.18). Corruption, in other words, is an integral part of the process of accumulation and social compromise.

We may well find attractive the argument that, prompted by a frustration with the limited channels through which power may be secured, corruption is the pursuit of political influence (and economic gain) in ways that have not been formalised or legitimised. But we must also accept that corruption is to be found within the older, stable, and formalised democracies where channels for political influence are multiple and comparatively open. And where again the prime motive force, argue Bicchieri and Duffy (1997), is the desire to increase or maintain political influence and financial gain. However, limits in the system lead us into a cycle of honesty and corruption. As the power of politicians increases, so their chances of being uncovered and penalised diminish, and corruption becomes more extensive. As time goes by both contractors (who are the sources of the politicians' pay-offs) and politicians demand larger and larger pay-offs. The politicians need larger and larger payoffs to consolidate their power because they are competing against other politicians whose income is rising, while the contractors need larger payoffs (income from contracts) to fund the increasing burden of bribes. All this time, however, the social costs are rising as monopoly prices and higher prices reduce the income of ordinary consumers. At some point, then, payoffs to contractors can no longer keep pace with bribes demanded by politicians. Both contractors and ordinary consumers, as they see their incomes fall, will now want to vote the politician out of office. In an effort to keep their contractors onside, politicians now begin to accept smaller and smaller bribes. The politicians have now, in effect, begun to draw on their stock of wealth to compensate contractors. Yet at some point the politicians will run out of money, and contractors will switch their allegiance to honest politicians under whom, in this more honest state, they will do comparatively better financially until - as contractors begin to offer bribes and politicians begin to accept - the cycle starts all over again.

We have, so far, suggested that corruption may be explained by the failure of structures to manage self-interest. A slightly different tack is to shift the burden of explanation squarely onto the structures themselves: they fail to manage self-interest *and* they are responsible for our self-interested attitude to the world. Williams (1976) makes this point quite explicit: without denying the significance of individual greed, it is clear that much corruption in the Third World is related to structural and institutional features, especially those which set the conditions in which government becomes the paramount source of goods, services and employment. Banfield (1970, 1975) also looks to institutions to explain our motivations. When it is the purpose of an organisation to maximise profit, then the question of corruption becomes one of costs and benefits. The costs of minimizing corruption may be high. Elaborate layers of monitorial procedures are expensive and bureaucratic, and are inimical to the organisation in other ways: employees feel spied upon and are robbed of initiative. But the rewards derived from corrupting the agents of other organisations - including their competitors, labour unions, and government - may also be high. This being so, then we might expect managers to calculate tolerance levels for internal and personal corruption (the sacrifice of the principal's interests in favour of its agents), and to weigh the benefits of external and official corruption (the violation of rules in order to serve the principal's interests) against its costs (such as financial or legal penalties, or a loss of reputation) in the event of discovery.

Government institutions differ from businesses in various ways. For instance, they have multiple aims and incentives. This means that often there is no attempt to balance costs and benefits: it is the duty of officials not to calculate levels of tolerance but to eradicate corruption altogether. On the other hand, uncertainties are built in: where authority is highly fragmented, where there is no system of monitoring and control, where officials are allowed discretionary powers, and where pay scales are inflexible, circumstances are created (namely weak centralising forces and too few agencies with which to enforce honesty [Banfield 1975, p.600]) in which the corrupt need only influence a segment of the government.

And, indeed, the degree of centralisation and decentralisation is, for many writers, of signal importance to an understanding of corruption. Some argue that in a decentralised state corruption is less likely: the dispersal of power will encourage more intense competition among politicians and departments (political and bureaucratic) for office and jurisdiction (functional and geographical), and closer monitoring of their activities. Thus opportunities and incentives for the extraction of rents will be reduced. Other writers, however, suggest that decentralisation will attract lower quality bureaucrats, encourage insular fiefdoms, reduce monitoring and coordination among bureaucrats, weaken accountability and, for these and other reasons, create opportunities and incentives for corruption. In support of these and other similar arguments, empirical evidence – most commonly in the form of correlations between corruption indexes and degrees of centralisation or decentralisation – can be found. For example, Fisman and Gatti (2002) argue that fiscal decentralisation and government expenditure is consistently associated with a lower incidence of corruption (perceived) among countries. The reason for this, they infer, is that greater decentralisation engenders greater accountability (p.327).

2.2 Multiple variables

For those writers who find these largely, or purely, economic or political interpretations of corruption a little too dry and monochrome, broader interpretations which are at once sociological, anthropological, economic, political and historical, but still largely structural, are felt to provide a more dimensional understanding of human behaviour and motivations. This broader view is indeed necessary, argues Cartier-Bresson (1997, p.465), if we are to move from an attempt to understand occasional and unorganised corruption in states which are otherwise thought to be healthy, to an understanding of states in which corruption is extensive and organised and, in these senses, normal. Cartier-Bresson's main concern is to elucidate how corruption is organised into pervasive networks or, as he puts it, 'how individual exits from the legal system are established and how such "treason" becomes organised into corruption networks' (p.466). His exposition comprises a number of parts or stages.

First, acts of corruption are normalised as gaps between the spoken order and the order of concrete hidden practices become common place. There is also a confusion of roles and functions (such as political with bureaucratic) and of motivations (such as the accumulation of money with prestige and recognition). In other words, multiple values and motivations are upheld and integrated. Secondly, systems of rights and obligations are first imposed on individuals, and then institutionalised. These begin to take priority over the individuals' obligations to the principal (such as the state or the firm). Eventually, individuals come to be defined by their own private networks, and will defend these before their own personal interests. Third, in the face of these 'priority' networks, the distinction between roles - such as bureaucrat and entrepreneur, or bureaucrat and citizen - is dissolved, most commonly into friendships. As roles blend and fuse, the internal and external boundaries of organisations become increasingly vague. Indeed, alliances between agents and third parties aim deliberately to soften - and to reduce their dependence on - the legal and organisational boundaries of their principals. Fourthly, with the dissolution of boundaries, networks accumulate a multiplicity of skills and activities. They also develop antechambers (such as social clubs) in which a potential member's reliability and competency can be tested. The forms and timing of payments now become increasingly complex, and supplies are centralised.

In effect Cartier-Bresson's model describes the fusion of the formal, informal, public, and private, and the blurring of economic, social, political and bureaucratic spheres of activity. But contained within this model are a number of assumptions from which causes may be inferred. For instance, there is heterogeneity of culture, resources and motivations – and this is said to lie at the base of corrupt exchange. (In particular, kernels – such as language, kinship, and place of origin - around which informal relationships may be established, provide a means and stimulus for corruption.) Economic, administrative, political, and social roles and activities are interconnected at a fundamental level. (More specifically, the different coordinating principles - market, hierarchy, and solidarity - for human activity are interdependent, so that each mobilises something of the other). The principles governing the regulation of informal and formal behaviour work together through a creative tension. And individual decisions are necessarily influenced by, and subordinated to, institutions: it is these which appear to have a hold over an individual's decision-making.

The implication of these arguments is that a tendency towards corrupt behaviour is probably inevitable. Values, actions, roles and motivations are multiple, dimensional, and hybrid; principles of coordination and of regulation (formal-informal) are mixed and interdependent; and the whole system is institutionalised spontaneously. All this, it seems, favours a move towards corruption which is, for those involved, natural, almost unnoticeable, and possibly moral.

A more common, though somewhat mechanical, approach to the analysis of multiple influences on corruption is to identify correlations among a range of variables which, though not universal, are found across many societies. Explanations are then inferred from these correlations. Treisman (2000), for example, identifies six variables: British Rule; Protestantism; exposure to democracy; federalism (and centralisation); economic development; and exports and openness (to trade). The key to understanding the interactions among these variables is the balance of costs and benefits that each offers to politicians and bureaucrats. Associated with each variable, therefore, are institutions, institutional patterns, and practices whose primary significance is that they raise or lower the costs and benefits for corrupt and honest behaviour.

The common law system associated with British Rule, Triesman argues, brings with it superior government. It emerged as a defence for parliament and property owners in England against the Crown's desire to expropriate and regulate. In contrast, the civil law systems which arose in, say, France and Germany were used by the sovereign to build the state and control economic life. Just as vital an influence on the efficacy of the legal system is the 'legal culture': 'conceptions of the social role of law and the relative importance of law in preserving the social order'...(p.402-3). Drawing on Ekstein (1966, p.265) Treisman argues that in Britain and in its former colonies, there is a tendency to 'behave like ideologists in regard to rules' and to treat procedures as 'sacred rituals' (cited in Treisman, p.403). In other countries, however, social order is associated not with a respect for procedure, but with a respect for hierarchy and the authority of office. Status and authority, in other words, take precedence over laws, rules, and procedures. In short, the common law - combined with an ideological or ritualistic treatment of laws, rules and procedures - make it more likely that corruption will be revealed even if this should offend hierarchy and authority.

A closely related variable is religion, for this, argues Treisman, conditions attitudes to the social hierarchy. Challenges to office-holders are rare where Catholicism, Eastern Orthodoxy and Islam dominate. Protestantism, however, is a more egalitarian and individualistic religion which tends to question the authority of the state, and places other citizens above family loyalty. Where Protestantism reigns, there exists a powerful and semi-revolutionary force working against nepotism, familism (Banfield, 1958) and the interests of state officials.

The risks which officials face are also much greater in a society with long exposure to democratic and open government. This is because there is greater freedom for association and for the press; civic participation is likely to be more vigorous; and competition for political office is more intense.

Economic development is also likely to work against corruption. This is so because it tends: to spread more widely education, literacy, and 'depersonalised' relationships; to clarify the boundaries among spheres of activity (public-private, economic, social, political and bureaucratic); and to stabilise the polity. Under such conditions it is more likely that corruption will be noticed and challenged; the value of bureaucrats' careers is raised (for their income is higher and their positions are relatively secure); and the stigma and shame associated with corruption is burdensome.

A busy and interventionist government which is quick to restrict foreign imports, limit competition, and allocate natural resources, will offer up protected markets with large and guaranteed incomes. This creates greater opportunities and incentives for corruption. Open markets will help to forestall such opportunities, eradicate incentives, and thereby reduce corruption.

Centralised government, as opposed to federal government, will also make corruption less likely. It does so by reducing the frequency of contacts with local officials whose influence within comparatively small geographical areas is relatively large, and through enforcement, anticorruption, auditing and other monitoring agencies which are able to provide coordinated oversight.

These six variables interact with each other in complex ways; and they are, for the most part, strongly associated with low levels of corruption. The more prevalent and deeply entrenched British rule, Protestantism, centralisation, openness, economic development, and democracy, the lower the levels of perceived corruption will be. It is not surprising, then, that fighting corruption proves to be so difficult, for the distant past, argues Treisman, 'appears as important as – or more important than – current policy. Democratisation has to be radical and long-lived and trade liberalisation has to be extensive to decrease corruption much. The one slightly more hopeful finding is that, even though corruption hinders growth, countries can at times grow their way out of corruption. If other factors lead to vigorous economic development, corruption is likely to decrease' (p.401-2). As far as economic development is concerned, there is a clear direction of causation from levels of economic development to corruption, and this relationship is robust and intense.

2.3 Criticisms

Despite their authority and popularity, structural explanations are open to various criticisms. And these lead us to ask just how far can an analysis of structures take us towards an understanding of corruption and its causes?

(i) One group of criticisms may be directed at those explanations which rely upon the identification of correlations. First, just how reliable are such data? We have already noted problems with perception indexes in chapter 1. We must also take on board the doubts which naturally surround much, if not all, of the statistical data that emerge from corrupt governments and agencies. Secondly, just what is the nature of the explanatory 'variables' that are identified? How sound is the assumption that they form discrete phenomena that interact in particular ways? Is this Cartesian view necessarily a helpful way of thinking about the social world?[*] Thirdly, these kinds of explanations do not amount to more than interpretations of correlations made in the light of certain assumptions including those which determine particular directions of cause and effect. For instance, we might argue that decentralisation, because of the dispersal of power and greater monitoring, leads to less corruption; but unless we can explain *why* this should be so, then other interpretations are left open to us. Fiscal decentralisation, as Fisman and Gatti (*op. cit.*) point out, may be selective: the funding of certain activities which attract high rents may be kept at the centre, while the funding for other activities which attract only low rents is decentralised. In other words there is an increase in decentralisation and a reduction in the incidence of corruption locally, precisely because politicians and bureaucrats at the centre are corrupt. Another possible interpretation of a correlation between decentralisation and reduced corruption is that a government may feel confident about decentralisation only if it believes that the level of corruption is already low, and that reliable sanctions (formal and informal) are in place. Decentralisation does not reduce corruption: it is an expression of low levels of corruption. The direction of cause and effect – if indeed such links exist – is by no means certain.

Similar questions surround Treisman's study. As we noted above, he argues that the level of corruption may be accounted for by the interaction of six variables, and that associated with each one are certain institutions, institutional patterns and practices which in the mind of officials raise or lower the costs and benefits of corruption. Thus for the variable 'British Rule' read the idealistic (even ritualistic) treatment of rules and procedures irrespective of office and status. For 'Protestantism' read 'egalitarianism' and a critical questioning of authority and

---

[*] These questions are considered in a little more depth in chapters 3 and 4.

jurisdiction. For 'democracy', read freedom to doubt, probe, participate and compete. For 'economic' development, read a strengthening ability to uncover corruption and the officials' deepening sense of shame when they are discovered to have breached the boundary between public and private spheres. For the last two variables – openness and centralisation – read more foreign trade, less government intervention, and greater oversight of a government's limited activities. Phrased in these ways, it is immediately apparent that many of the institutions, institutional patterns, and practices associated with each variable – such as the freedom to probe and compete, clearly defined public and private spheres, depersonalised relationships, and the ritualistic treatment and equal application of rules and procedures irrespective of status, office, and kinship – are very close to what are commonly regarded as honest and proper behaviour. In other words, these variables do not so much explain as describe propriety. It is hardly surprising, therefore, that there should be strongly positive correlations between these variables and the low incidence of corruption. By the same token, the absence of these variables - and the prevalence of, say, a lack of competitive freedom and openness, weak oversight of frequent contacts between merchants and officialdom, and the subordination of rules and procedures to hierarchy, office, and kinship – would seem to describe, rather than explain, high levels of corruption.

(ii) A more general criticism which can be made of structural explanations is that they always seem to leave us with yet one more step to make. Let us for the moment accept that in some cases decentralisation (through the dispersal of power, greater competition, and a strengthening of monitoring and accountability) may reduce the opportunities and incentives for corruption; and that, following decentralisation, levels of corruption do fall. Let us also accept that, in other cases, greater centralisation (with its demands for higher quality bureaucrats, more effective coordination, and better oversight) may also reduce the opportunities and incentives for corruption; and that, following centralisation, levels of corruption also fall. Let us now ask if we have yet managed to explain corruption? We have identified the institutional conditions in which levels of corruption seem to rise or fall. But the more important question remains unanswered: what is it about people that they should act corruptly either in the presence or absence of such institutional arrangements? Why should they be corruptible in the absence of dispersed power, competition and monitorial procedures and institutions; why should they be corruptible because they are not 'high quality' or because coordination is poor? If there is an inherent tendency to become corrupt unless certain institutional conditions are met, then why is this so?

We may also wish to accept Treisman's suggestions that the fair and equal application of laws, rules, and procedures, may raise the cost and reduce the incidence of corruption. But if we are to explain corruption, we must first answer a number of questions. Why are rules and procedures treated properly, and fairly applied? Why is freedom valued? Why are the public and private spheres clearly defined? Why are relationships depersonalised (if indeed they are)? Similarly, if it is true that the costs and benefits of corruption are raised when, say, rules and procedures are subordinated to hierarchy and family, and when freedom and competition are curtailed, then why are those features present? Treisman goes no further than to leave an explanation outside the door of culture and history. Consequently, the reasons occasionally given for the significance of the variables identified are not always very convincing. For instance, is Protestantism really so individualistic, and is Islam really only state-supporting? And are 'the British' really bound so tightly to their rules and procedures?

Bicchieri and Duffy's model, too, merely assumes that politicians want to increase their own power and income; that all of them are prepared to act corruptly; and that honesty on the part of contractors is largely a function of cost. There is no attempt to explore why politicians should want power and money, why they should be prepared to act corruptly, or why contractors are only likely to act honestly on the grounds of cost. We should say in defence of the model that (like all models) it makes all kinds of assumptions (including those of consistency), many of which are probably unsupportable; and that the model's authors are aware of this. Their intention is to illustrate the principles underlying a cycle, and not to explain corruption. Yet is it possible to illustrate the principles if we cannot explain them? The fact is that we are left wondering why politicians and contractors are predisposed to act corruptly. If the argument is that surrounding structures have led them into a state of corruption, then why is this so?

We might say much the same of Khan's explanation. He describes the structures which produce corrupt behaviour (or behaviour which may be interpreted as corrupt), but he does not explain why the structures are so well organised and focussed on growth in South Korea, Malaysia and Thailand, and not so well focussed in India. Why do politicians, bureaucrats and merchants organise their relationships and practices in the way that Khan describes?

One response which might be made to this general criticism - that structural explanations seem unfinished - is to refer back to the assumption often made: that people are either motivated by self-interest or (though for some readers this will amount to the same thing) they are fundamentally corrupt. Yet this reply still leaves unexplained this base quality of human nature, and it presents us with a further awkward question. If it is human nature to be self-interested and corrupt, then how is it that institutions and practices capable of checking and constraining such powerful instincts are able to form and remain honest? Is there, perhaps, something about the way in which people behave collectively that is different from the way in which they behave as individuals?

Another response which might be made is that human nature is fundamentally good; or (though again for some readers this will amount to the same thing) that the pursuit of self-interest is quite proper, and entirely moral, behaviour.

Yet this reply, too, leaves unexplained our goodness and why, therefore, imperfections in our institutions and practices should arise.

Yet another response might be to refer back to the argument that it is our institutions which are responsible for our motivations and our fundamental goodness or dishonesty. But this reply still leaves us wondering about how those institutions arose in the first place and what motivated the people who established them? We are also left asking, yet again, how did corruption emerge from institutions that generate fundamentally honest people, and how are honest institutions established and sustained if the individuals they shape are fundamentally dishonest?

3.0 Cultural explanations

Dissatisfaction with the sense of incompleteness which attends structural explanations may be one important reason why some writers believe that we need to take a closer look at culture. We have noted that many discussions on one or more combination of variables at some point ask the reader to consider in very general terms the role of cultural factors and their historical evolution. Other writers are determined to explore cultural influences more thoroughly. We noted earlier Rose-Ackerman's argument that corruption may be understood as the mismanagement of self-interest and that this, for the most part, takes on structural forms. In addition to these economic and political structural features she considers the question of culture.

> 'In societies with embedded interpersonal networks, citizens may care little about market and public sector efficiency. They may view impersonal markets as illegitimate and morally bankrupt.....People may believe they should give freely to others in their family or group and expect that "gifts" will be made in return....Trade, for them, is legitimate only with particular partners on the other side of the transaction. A society based on such highly personalised relations will have difficulty developing large-scale capitalist enterprise or supporting active cross-border trade...' (p.106).

Imposing new and formal institutions in this context may produce a virtuous circle, as the benefits which accrue to those operating within a modern and differentiated sector begin to persuade others to try it out. But vicious circles are also possible. Ill-fitting institutions throw up pathologies which make gradual changes in attitude less likely as people observe the costs of markets and bureaucracies.

> 'Payoffs to state officials may be common; many market trades may be based on personal connections; and state purchases and personnel appointments may continue to be part of a web of patronage. On the one hand, the market may lose its fragile legitimacy by intruding into areas where it is viewed as illegitimate even in developed market economies. On the other hand, the market may have difficulty becoming established even in those areas where it produces clear efficiency gains...' (p.108).

Many parts of Africa, for example, face a crisis of institutions 'mainly due to a structural and functional disconnect, or lack of convergence, between formal institutions that are mostly transplanted from outside and informal institutions that are rooted in African history, tradition and culture and that generally characterise the governance of civil society' (Dia, 1996, p.29, cited in Rose-Ackerman, p.109).

Nevertheless, culture is far from being a deterministic force: culture can be managed. People in developing countries *do* make a distinction between appropriate and inappropriate behaviour, and cultures *do* change. And it may often be that manageable structural features are, for one reason or another, mistakenly presented as problems of culture. For Rose-Ackerman there is a fairly simple way to test whether or not cultural influences are too deeply rooted to be handled effectively. If certain kinds of behaviour (such as gift-giving) which might be regarded by outsiders as corrupt are indeed accepted within a given culture, then that behaviour should be practiced openly and potential hidden costs should be allowed to come to light. If, as a consequence, attitudes to that practice should change, then either it is a manageable cultural problem, or it has been a manageable structural problem all long.

Take, for example, the 'morally-loaded' terms of price, gift, bribe, and tip. Whilst gift exchange is a major social norm in developing countries, Rose-Ackerman suggests that it is possible to make distinctions among these four terms based on who the payment is made to, and on whether or not there exists any explicit *quid pro quo*. Thus price = payment to a principal + an explicit *quid pro quo*; gift = payment to a principal (with no explicit *quid pro quo*); bribe = payment to agent + explicit *quid pro quo*; tip = payment to agent (with no explicit *quid pro quo*). Pervasive bribery indicates not the working out of gift-exchange or some other cultural determinant, but the inefficient structuring of a society's agency relationships. If this is right, then relationships will be made more efficient, and bribery will quickly evaporate, if, say, customers openly hire agents to deal with their old principals. In practical terms this means, for example, a further privatisation of state functions.

The failure to make a clear distinction between bribes and gifts, then, is an example of mismanagement. It gives license to bribery and allows individuals who engage in bribery to build up a reputation for generosity towards those who help them. Other examples of mismanagement include: poor law enforcement (this makes it easier to establish a reputation in the first place); the entrenchment of small local markets (in which producers deal with the government frequently); unequal punishment of bribers and bribees (officials are easily held to ransom by a businessman if, on discovery, an official is to suffer the harsher penalty); toleration of closed circles of reciprocal obligations (in which the subtle and long-term exchange of favours becomes established); and the provision of ineffective mechanisms to deal with legal disputes quickly and at low cost.

Structural analyses of the Philippines have also been sensitive to the role of culture. Kerkvliet (1995) argues that whilst the patron-client framework is deservedly influential, analyses should move beyond it and develop a more textured view of the Philippines' polity. In its broad historical and structural sweep,

Hutchcroft's patrimonial analysis does meet this concern to some extent. But other more radical variants and alternatives have been suggested (Thompson, 1995; Wurfel, 1988). Putzel (1999), by marrying institutional analysis with the concept of social capital, attempts to uncover those underlying cultural features which may explain why the Philippines is a weak or shallow democracy. By shallow it is meant that the Philippines meets only to a minimal extent the defining qualities of democracy – free and regular elections, universal suffrage, freedom of expression, the flow of accurate information, associational autonomy, and the rule of law effected by an impartial judiciary. The 'depth', or shallowness, of democracy, depends upon what North (1990) calls the informal institutions, and what Putzel describes as the cultural features (such as customs, traditions, and codes of conduct), that partly govern behaviour in state, society and economy. These features – in combination with the social capital (the trust, norms and networks) which accrue from familial relationships – are held to explain shifting coalitions of clan power, the appearance of regionally-based language groups, the exchange of votes for favours, the granting of public contracts to cronies, and other problems with the Philippine polity. There are similarities between this interpretation and Landé's (1965); but whereas Landé saw little sign or hope of change, Putzel, by the end of the century, saw evidence of a deepening of democracy. And in this process, civic associations – whose members promote democratic norms and values, and are independent of the state – may have a vital role. These associations, as they gather around the existing democratic framework, may act as a vigorous stimulus for change. Landé (2001), too, though cautious, later appeared to see indications of change in a polity now groping to strike a balance 'among the rights of the citizenry, the rights of public officials, and the needs of public institutions' (p. 101).

We have argued so far that dissatisfaction with a sense of incompleteness surrounding structural explanations is one reason for turning to culture. But there is another and, for many writers, a more important reason: the structural explanation - where it is used to provide explanations across cultures and where corruption is understood as a departure from western formalism - is decidedly ethnocentric. It is to analyse the world through a mind shaped by western formalism. The structural approach, argue Haller and Shore (2005) merely lists "corruption" with so many other negative characteristics such as 'underdeveloped', 'poor', 'ignorant', 'repressive', 'fundamentalist', 'fanatical', 'irrational', 'transitional', 'developing', and 'other'. With its moral and evolutionary overtones, the structural approach portrays corruption as a symptom of the social pathology of Third World societies; it is a colonial thesis about 'primitive' and 'savage' countries. Even the more positive structural arguments are roundly criticised: the suggestion that corruption simply 'fills the gaps' left by weak states and may help those societies become modern and rational is hardly credible. How can it be, they wonder with Sampson (1983, p.72), that corruption 'encourages capital formation and entrepreneurship, diminishes red tape, mitigates ethnic conflicts, integrates pariah groups into society, and gives more people a stake in the system' (cited in Haller and Shore *op. cit.*, p.4).

These criticisms emerge from a more intense and more self-conscious form of cultural explanation - one that is described as an anthropological perspective. Its adherents believe themselves to be more aware of, and more concerned with, the subtle inflections of behaviour and thought which, they feel, are deeply rooted in the cultural and structural qualities peculiar to different societies and groups. Conventional definitions of, and approaches towards, corruption may make a distinction between public and private spheres of life: the violation of the one by the other finds expression as corruption. But in fact, argue Haller and Shore, the

'public-private dichotomy is often an arbitrary and inherently ambiguous cultural category. As Gupta's (1995) analysis of state officials in northern India illustrates, Western assumptions about the rational activity of office-holders simply do not translate. The distinction between an official's role as public servant and private citizen is collapsed, not only as the site of their activity, but also in their styles of operation' (p.5).

This collapse of the public and the private, then, is not held to be symptomatic of backwardness, traditionalism, and underdevelopment. Nor is it understood to reinforce what is described as the conventional belief that corruption emerges from the confusion of the public and the private. This quality, the absence of a public-private distinction, is simply 'not western'. One striking conclusion which follows from this is that western social scientists, western governments, and western agencies, 'see' the problem of corruption only because they have a particularly western 'cultural category' – that of formalism – locked into their heads. And it is only when this category is drawn into practice that difficulties begin. 'Corruption', it would seem, is only a problem when viewed through a mind imbued with western formalism, and when that mind imposes itself upon the non-western. If we were able to free ourselves of this category, we would begin to see beyond 'corruption', and begin to comprehend the complex and nuanced 'ritual', 'conversation', 'poem', 'narratives', 'forms of exchange', or - as in the practice of Chinese *guanxi* - the 'art' which bind together individuals and state, and allow us to make sense of the world (Vivanathan and Sethi, 1998; Zinn, 2001; Yang, 1994). To interpret this sophisticated, fluid, dimensional and finely graduated context of gifts, bartering, moral codes, networks, and narratives, through a clumsy, clanking, and mechanistic concept such as corruption, does not help us to understand society, nor does it do society any good.

Viewed through this glass, the deepening concern and interest in corruption - and in the apparent rise in its incidence and extent - is a product of western cultural categories. A still less charitable view is that such concerns are part and parcel of attempts by neo-liberals to reduce the size of the public sector and to subject remaining public servants to the demands of business and entrepreneurial practices. It is, in other words, a new stick with which to beat non-western governments until they comply with the economic and political agenda of the US and the dictates of global capitalism (Haller and Shore, *op. cit.*, p.19).

3.1 Criticisms

The notion that corruption is a western concept, and that it emerges as a problem with the imposition of western formalism, is of some importance. But it is an argument that needs heavy qualification, and for a number of reasons.

(i) Cultural relativism provides easy justification for those who wish to act in ways that are detrimental to others. Furthermore, if there is a need for formal institutional practices and loyalties, and for the separation of professional and social spheres, then perceptions and behaviour which weaken those practices, undermine those loyalties, and dissolve the distinction between spheres of activity, are at best unhelpful and at worst damaging. A question of more interest, and which is more difficult to answer, is whether a strict adherence to the formal patterns of behaviour and loyalties set by institutions necessarily produce a more stable, tolerant, and efficient society?

(ii) It is difficult to argue convincingly that formal institutional behavior (and the separation of professional and social spheres) is peculiarly western or modern, or that informal non-institutional behavior (and the blurring of professional and social spheres) is peculiarly non-western or traditional. There is also something unsatisfactory about the suggestion that formalised institutional behaviour is conditioned by 'western' culture. For unless we can distinguish between cultural features on the one hand, and, on the other, the formalised behaviour which those features are said to produce, then we are left with a circular and empty argument.

(iii) A very similar problem attends the suggestion that cultures peculiar to non-western societies condition the emergence of informal societies in which there is little or no distinction between public and private spheres of action. But in this case we are also left with the intriguing suggestion that non-western societies are produced by cultures which are (to the extent that they perpetuate and condition informality) predictable and impersonal in nature - qualities which would seem to indicate a degree of formality. The suspicion which arises now is that the whole debate - on the extent to which a formal or informal view of the world is peculiar to different societies - tells us more about social science than it does about the world we study. Could it not be the case that western and non-western societies may be just as formal or informal as each other? Formality, we might argue, simply describes what is accepted and regularised, while informality describes the unacceptable and, therefore, the irregular and uncertain. Social scientists, it might be argued, are often unfamiliar with the fine details of those unspoken practices and those inflections of behaviour and speech which make up the accepted, the regular, and the predictable within the communities in which they are interested. This is so because nowadays scholars commonly spend far more of their time in their universities than they ever do in the field. They move quickly between study site, conference hall and lecture theatre, and rarely have the opportunity to live year after year among the people they study. Moreover, social scientists are compelled by their training, by the expectations of their profession, and by lack of time, to rely on their highly formalised modes of thought and procedure to elucidate, to explain and to understand. These thought patterns find most obvious expression through concepts such as culture, structure, and categories of discrete phenomena which are held to describe, direct and explain human behaviour. Where it is the case that their subjects draw upon similar formalised patterns of thought (or even upon some version of the social scientists' own concepts) and, therefore, where their subjects' behaviour coincides with the social scientists' expectations, then the world revealed to social scientists is one formalised in quality. In this event, the social scientists' concepts - which are often passed back and forth between social scientists and their subjects - may take on a kind of explanatory value. But where the thought and behaviour of social scientists and their subjects is not synchronized, then social scientists (and this is no less true of those who adhere to an 'anthropological perspective') see only difference and informality. Social science, when it is blind to the formality around it, interprets what is believed to be informality through its own formalised trains of thought, throwing up conflicting visions: of societies boiling with greed, selfishness and childish chaos; of numinous societies disturbed by hard-nosed western ambition; of societies traditional or in transition; or of societies that are simply and quintessentially different.

4.0 Conclusions

There is, however, a more fundamental criticism that we can level at the cultural explanation: how do we explain the particular cultural traits which, it is claimed, explain the features and behaviour that lead either to corruption or to practices which are interpreted as being corrupt? If the structural explanation takes us only so far, then can we not say the same thing about the cultural explanation? Are we not forced at some point to turn to structures to explain the genesis or perpetuation of cultural elements? Might we not also argue (and this is implied above in section 3.1 [ii] above) that the structures of the social scientists' own profession condition their analyses of culture?

Any attempt to frame an explanation of corruption around a choice between culture and structure is beginning to seem very hollow. It appears, even from this very brief and selective review, that neither approach on its own is likely to produce a satisfactory explanation of corruption: just as structure looks to culture, so culture looks to structure.

CHAPTER 3
The Causes of Corruption:
structural-cultural dialectics and social change

1.0 Introduction

In the previous chapter we suggested that there appears to be a symbiotic or dialectical relationship between cultural and structural explanations of corruption. This present chapter goes on to illustrate this dialectic through a consideration of a debate on factionalism in China. Here, Ting Gong (1997) argues, market driven reforms and decentralisation have reshuffled economic power, shifting more of it into the hands of officials lower down the political and bureaucratic hierarchy while opening up countless opportunities for them to make money. To explain the political and bureaucratic features of economic reform is to explain the relationships, networks, and factional groupings of officials at all levels. And this requires an understanding of these features' structural and cultural dimensions. But does the burden of explanation rest with structure or with culture?

2.0 A structural-cultural dialectic

Nathan's original factional model - which, as Nathan and Tsai (1995) point out, have been found useful by scholars 'as a starting point for analysing how China's political elite works' - was intended as a structural argument. However, a criticism frequently made of it was that 'it did not succeed in distinguishing between cultural and structural (or institutional) variables... many scholars agreed that things often happened in China the way the factionalism model described, but felt uncomfortable explaining these patterns in terms of either structure or culture. This quandary relates more broadly to the traditional polarisation of cultural and structural approaches in China studies: the respective independent variables are presented as mutually exclusive, yet they are hard to distinguish. And neither cultural nor structural arguments alone seem to carry sufficient explanatory power' (p.158-60).

Nathan and Tsai then set out what they mean by culture and structure. Throughout the social sciences, they note, structure tends to be thought of

'as patterns of incentives outside actors' heads and culture as attitudes, values, and beliefs inside actors' heads. From an actors' point of view, structure is a situation (or part of it) and culture a set of attitudes (or some of them) that he or she brings to the situation. Structure in this sense is thought to impose the exogenous discipline of means-end rationality on actors, while culture is the source of values that are not determined by structure and are in this sense non- (or pre-) rational' (p.161).

However, while certain technological, ecological and geographic realities may create incentive structures that are exogenous to culture,

'in political life most structures are created by actors who are also the bearers of culture. That is, political institutions represent products of human interaction, which itself is culturally conditioned. Certainly this is the case with the scenarios described by the factionalism model. In these situations, structures...are partly derivative of culture if only because participants are able to understand these rules and accept them as legitimate; and culture in turn is shaped partly by socialisation to existing patterns of incentives – that is, to structures. Hence, structure and culture are not only socially construc6ed but also mutually constitutive in the Geertzian sense. Most of the criticism of the factionalism model flow from this failure to clarify the relationship between culture and structure....' (p.163).

Nathan and Tsai attempt to clarify the relationship between culture and structure: whilst human interaction defines both culture and structure, institutions, once created, become an objective reality to actors who manoeuvre within their boundaries. While they do not rule out cultural influences, and while they accept that structure and culture are mutually constituted, they also contend that

> 'once they take shape as everyday, taken-for-granted reality, institutions provide an objective basis for substantially structuring behaviour. While institutions have historical roots, they can be treated as if they were relatively autonomous at a given point in time in the way they affect the choices of individuals acting in social situations (p.167-8).

In other words, whatever the causes of institutions (and there may be a cultural element in this), institutions, from the point of view of actors, are real and do shape behaviour and thus they may be said to have effects.

In an attempt to demonstrate the practical value of these ideas, Nathan and Tsai put together a revised factional model. They envisage four sets of associational bases (kinship, community, agreement and exchange-based participation) and four sets of communication patterns (hierarchical, segmentary, noded dyadic and open network). Together these combine to produce certain types of groups (16 in all). Each exhibits certain types of behaviour in accordance with particular attributes which are inherent in those associations and patterns of communications. Upon this, rules are layered to form an operational *millefeuille*. There is, for instance, the rule that choices are defined in substantial part by the institutional environs; and there are rules which govern the link between the types of associational base and channels of communication, the motivations and organisational abilities of those groups, and the political behaviour of those groups. For example, there is the rule that community-based hierarchical groups are capable of organising specialised armed force and of conducting elaborate military expeditions; the rule that kinship has roughly equal portions of 'type of end'; the rule that community-motivated action is more 'psychological' and 'group-regarding'; and the rule that exchange-based groups are least willing to take risks because their 'ends' are predominantly 'material' and 'self-regarding'.

Of central importance are the type 15 (exchange-based, noded) groups, for these go together to make up factions. Exchange-based participation, write Nathan and Tsai, 'is motivated by the individual's pursuit of relatively tangible and immediate incentives, such as money, goods, office or protection. This includes both short-term, socially disvalued or neutrally valued exchanges such as pay-offs or log-rolling and relatively well-established, persistent, socially valued patterns of exchange such as "clientelism" (p.171-2). And a noded-dyadic pattern is described as one 'in which communications are transmitted through a network of two-person links, but are disproportionately routed through certain individuals, who thus stand at the foci or nodes of the network. Groups with this communication pattern are likely to have unclear membership boundaries. Yet they are internally differentiated, since the persons standing at the communications nodes have greater power and are perceived as leaders.' (p.173). Factions occur 'in villages, bureaucracies, legislatures, or other settings when a leader mobilises a set of followers (who may in turn mobilise their own followers) to support him or her on the basis of expected rewards of office, influence or money. Due to their flexibility, factions can engage in a wide variety of tactics. But since they are limited in size and follower commitment, they do not challenge the status quo. An isolated corrupt pay-off would also belong to this type, paralleling the old boys' network and cooperation among kin as ways for an individual to mobilize influence through personal connexion' (pp.179-80).

How, then, is the emergence of factions to be explained? The model presents us with certain conditions and rules for the production of factions. But how and why does the model work in the ways that its creators say? What are the general forces setting and enforcing those conditions and rules? Nathan and Tsai argue that whilst an institutional approach begs a cultural explanation as much as the cultural approach begs an institutional one, culture is not the only cause and its explanatory role is limited.

'Certain patterns of belief and action that some analysts treat as cultural can be better explained by reference to organised situations that actors face. Since culture and structure are mutually constituted, institutions can be said to have cultures. A given political action, say an episode of factional manoeuvring, is for the actors at once a decision adopted from within a set of attitudes and a choice taken with an eye to an institutionalised situation. "Bases for association" are at once attributes or organisations and value commitments that motivate individual action....[But] at a given moment, institutions confront their participants in the form of incentives and disincentives, possibilities and impossibilities, and prudential and normative rules. These influence behaviour in addition to, apart from, and in many respects more than, the concurrent influence of culture.' (p.189)

Culture and structure are mutually constituted: structures are created by actors who are also bearers of culture; and both structures and culture are the product of human interaction. Yet when individuals are faced with institutions and institutional situations as a given moment in time, those institutions take shape as everyday taken-for-granted reality; structure becomes analytically disguisable from culture, as the one precipitates out of the other.

What catalyst permits this reaction, such that it now becomes possible to separate the institutions from the behaviour they yield, from their underlying bases and communication patterns, and from their cause? What is it that transforms institutions (in this case, factions) into objective realities and separates out cause from effect? No answer is given, though it may lie with those factors which Nathan and Tsai believe to be more important than culture: the environing institutions (such as the bureaucratic and electoral system), economic change, war, international events or historical conjunctures.

In a very real sense, however, the origin of factions is neither here nor there: it is the reality of the effects of factional behaviour, especially on the reproduction of behaviour, which matters. The very operation of factions constitutes the structures that shape behaviour and reproduce factions.

Other writers do not find this kind of argument very satisfactory. They prefer to look to culture. Dittmer (1995) envisages a model of Chinese politics comprising two kinds of relationships: the purpose-rational (those which are a means to an end); and the value-rational (those valued as ends in themselves). The purpose-rational are:

> 'typically formed with those colleagues, subordinates and superiors with whom one has routine occupational contacts. These relationships may be mobilised in support of career objectives so long as they are in the collective interests of the organisation of which all are a part; thus we may refer to this ensemble of occupational relationships as one's *formal base*. By mobilizing one's formal base one is able to exert official power which the Chinese refer to as *quanli* (p.10, italics in original).

Value-rational relationships comprise 'an informal "political base"... on the basis of which one can exercise informal power, or *shili*. A political base may be measured in terms of its *depth* and *breadth*: a "broad" base consists of a network of cronies located throughout the party, military, diplomatic, and governmental apparatus, whereas a "deep" base consists of supporters going all the way back to the early generation of the revolutionary leadership, hence having high seniority and elevated positions' (Dittmer, 1995, p.12, italics in original).

This informal political base is put together 'though the incremental accretion of discrete "connections". People have a large but finite number of potential affinities, including kinship, common geographic origin, former classmates, teachers or students, or common Field Army affiliation – at least one of which is usually necessary to form a connection (*guanxi*). A cadre assigned to a new task or post will immediately canvass an area for such objective affinities as a priority *sine qua non* objective, not just wait for them to emerge haphazardly' (*ibid.*).

The relationship between informal and formal politics is fluid and ambiguous, but may be understood to throw up particular features. Informality tends to be dominant, while formal politics often provides no more than a façade; individuals establish formal bases more as fall-backs in the event their informal bases (and their patrons) should weaken or be removed; and while the formal members of the elite are supposed to be equal, there is among them an informal hierarchy of patron-client relationships.

The explanation of these qualities is essentially cultural. Chinese culture, Dittmer argues, is neither individualistic nor group oriented but 'relationship based'; and Chinese attributes (such as kinship, classmate and school ties) 'may articulate into vast networks', and may also be defined by 'fixed frames' (such as family, village and workplace). We also learn that 'the need for hierarchy has deep cultural roots' and that the 'implicit cultural model for China's elite politics is the imperial court system, the role of the emperor being played by what Deng called the Party "core", but which we term the "Supreme Leader" (Dittmer, *op. cit.* pp. 20 and 19).

However, the extent to which informality or formality becomes more prominent and features of the polity alter, depends upon many things including, in particular, structural circumstances. While informal politics remains more potent in China than in other countries (and is likely to remain so), 'the historical trend it to formalisation' (Dittmer, *op. cit.* p.18). This is especially true since the death of Mao, for the 'overall thrust of development since the advent of political reform....has been towards increasing formalisation, as measured by the frequency, length and regularity of meeting sessions, and the number of people or procedural stages involved in drafting legislation' (Dittmer, *op. cit.* p.17). The secularisation of Mao Zedong thought, Deng's pragmatic focus on growth, and 'the attendant dismissal of the spectre of an elite "struggle between two lines" and "people in the party taking the capitalist road", have reduced the ideological barriers to the operation of factions (Dittmer, *op. cit.* pp.30-31). Combined with an easing of disciplinary measures against officials, and with attempts both to legalise their tenure and to restore popular respect for officialdom, the ebbing of ideology has allowed factional behaviour to become somewhat less clandestine. Elite factions have now begun to pursue and to represent the interests of their constituencies. In the wake of reform, elite coalitions have even begun to move away from 'factions' towards 'policy groups', the next stage being the formal structures and formal alliances which make up a 'bureaucratic' polity.

Encouraged by structural circumstances, then, the strengthening of purpose-rational (instrumental) relationships has (from a certain point of view) had a favourable influence on China's polity. Such relationships have led to greater formalisation and even to pluralism in a state where 'the diminution in the relative importance of ideology has led leaders to resort to formal-legal rationality as the most potent available means of legitimization' (*ibid.*). There is, now, a growing institutionalisation of various bureaucratic systems at all but the highest levels; the reliance on explicit rules and procedures is increasing; informal groups, now oriented more towards policies designed to enhance bureaucratic interests, are being transformed into professional, vocational, business and pressure groups – and even, as in the case of the reformists and conservatives, into quasi-parties. Of course, few things are certain: as a political form, 'informal politics...tends to be progressive in terms of policy, as its flexibility facilitates more rapid change by offering short-cuts to standard bureaucratic procedures [and] this has helped make China an extraordinarily well-led country compared to others in the Third World (albeit not always wisely governed)' (*ibid.*). Moreover, informal politics in China tends to 'reinforce traditional hierarchical relationships (including the "cult" of leadership inherited from the empire), and culturally embedded relationships more generally (for instance, time honoured primordial "connections") at the expense of rational-legal and meritocratic arrangements' (Dittmer, *op. cit.* p.33). But structural circumstances may also work to alter the basic cultural components of informal-formal politics:

> 'the overall decline in the status of ideology...and the increasing importance of purpose-rational relationships seems to have had both an emancipatory and

corrosive impact upon guanxi – emancipatory because with the relaxation of constraints on lateral communication brought about by the end of the class struggle and the spread of the market, contacts of all types are multiplying. At the same time the reform's impact is corrosive in the sense that such connexions have become suffused with utilitarian consideration. As a consequence, the dichotomy ...between value-rational and purpose-rational relationships has tended to break down. A new type of connection has emerged that is more instrumental and less sentimental' (p.29).

2.1 Doubts?

Structural and cultural explanations ask us to make shifts in emphasis, not exclusive choices. The one cannot do without the other. But should we be content to accept the suggestion that culture and structure are mutually constituted? Or does the circular nature of the argument indicate that something is wrong - that we have reached an impasse? When we reach out and begin to close our hand around the answer, it vanishes, only to reappear somewhere else. And as we run here and there clutching at the air, the fear grows that we are playing with our own shadow, and that we need to re-think how it is that we think about the social world.

A response to this criticism is that culture and structure cannot emerge anew with each generation. If they had to be re-invented there would be next-to-no development. Whatever the original explanation of culture, and whatever the original explanation of structure, the truth is that, here and now, structure and culture each influence and shape the other. There is little to be gained from scratching around in search of their ultimate origins. It is an understanding of their mutual influence that will help us to understand human societies.

Let us accept this defence for the moment, and put aside our doubts. The structural-cultural dialectic, we are sure, will do the job. The problem lies not here in this dialectic, but with a tendency to view corruption as a specific (and often uni-dimensional) phenomenon rather than as an interpretation of many expressions of our dimensional behaviour. As we serve up for analysis 'corruption' and its causes and effects, we must force ourselves to abstract elements of behaviour from their wider context. Inevitably we begin to isolate; we focus *either* on culture *or* on structure; and soon we find ourselves turning back and forth between the two as we attempt to uncover their origins and put together a complete explanation. The solution is to resist this tendency; to view culture and structure as genuinely interdependent phenomena which must be considered together; and to leave within their broad organic context those elements of behaviour which we would otherwise have abstracted to form the cultural or structural features of 'corruption'. The task we now face - to achieve an understanding of that organic context - may be far more demanding, yet far more rewarding. With this end in mind, we would do well to start with the question of social change.

3.0 Social change

As we turn to the notion of social change, we are drawn into the core of social theory and asked to range across many disciplines from sociology and anthropology to philosophy and economics. In this literature the key to understanding social change is commonly thought to lie with an understanding of the increasing complexity of structure. Yet the dialectic or symbiosis between structure (the norms, values and meanings conditioning behaviour) and culture (the learned aspects of human behaviour and, at a deeper sub-conscious level, our language, grammar and patterns of thought) is clear.

The notion of structure, and ideas about its evolving complexity, owe much to the science of biology. Society is understood, like an organism, to comprise mutually dependent parts or structures with specific functions. Society's increasing complexity describes the growth and differentiation of its interdependent parts or, in other words, its functional solidarity. For Compte (d.1857) the prime mover of social change was the law of three stages – the progress of human knowledge from a theological state (in which phenomena were explained by a fictitious being); through a metaphysical state (in which explanations looked to abstract but imaginary entities); to a scientific or positive state (in which there is an attempt to discover 'the actual law of phenomena'). For him, the unstable revolutionary crises of during late 18th century and the opening of the 19th century were symptomatic of the confusion generated by the co-existence of these incompatible states.

Spencer (d.1903), too, understood society as an organism, but one whose structural differentiation is driven by competition between societies. In its turn, differentiation produces changes in the form of cooperation. Spontaneous or individual cooperation (which operates in a market economy) gradually replaces compulsory or militant cooperation - terms which describe how individual wills are constrained, shaped, and directed by the group and its regulatory agencies. This change in the form of cooperation takes place because it is not possible to coordinate increasingly complex interactions through coercion. Instead, a flexible trading system is required. Evolution, however, is not inevitable, though the maintenance of militant cooperation will leave society at a moral and competitive disadvantage.

In his understanding of social evolution, Durkheim (d.1917) also envisaged two kinds of society: a more simple, undifferentiated, and segmented entity (described as mechanical solidarity); and a more complex entity (described as organic solidarity) in which individuals take on different social roles. The shift from mechanical to organic is promoted by increases in the volume and density of society. At the heart of this distinction lay two forms of consciousness.

> 'The one comprises only states that are personal to each of us, characteristic of us as individuals, while the other comprises states that are common to the whole of society. The former represents only our individual personality, which it constitutes; the latter represents the collective type and...the society without which it would not exist' (Durkheim, 1984, p.61).

Durkheim later replaced 'collective consciousness' with 'collective representations' – a term which he used to refer to ideas which helped to order and make sense of the world. These representations, he argued, emerged from groups, but then took on an autonomous existence. It is these collective representations that dominate and hold together a segmented society. In a state of organic solidarity, however, where individual consciousness dominates, society is held together largely by the practical demands which attend the sharpening division of labour, and by a kind of civil religion that supplies the common principles and justification for individualism. But as individualism and the fissures deepen, society comes to be characterised by *anomie* - a condition of moral de-regulation produced by the isolation of the individuals. The remedy, in Durkheim's view, is to establish local groups (such as occupational guilds or cooperatives); and to turn the central authority into an organ responsible for manufacturing the collective representations through which the various local groups can be coordinated and held together.

For Durkheim, the individual was subordinate to collective representations - to the structures of society which existed autonomously of, and could not be reduced to, the individual. This was the norm; a society in which individuals no longer conformed to the collective consciousness should be considered as abnormal. By contrast, Weber – who argued that the social world could not be analysed with methods and concepts applicable to the natural world, and for whom the proper subject of study was the social action of one or more individuals – social phenomena *could* be reduced to the behaviour of individual human beings. He suggested four categories of ideal forms of social actions: traditional actions (actions performed because they always had been); affectional action (acts driven by emotion); value- rational action; and end-rational (or instrumental) action. An increase in rationality (value-rational and end-rational actions) characterised the development of modern societies, and found expression through, say, the capitalistic organisation of labour and the organisation of large bureaucracies (systems of administration with clearly defined roles and tasks, and populated by qualified and salaried staff who were appointed and promoted on merit). The consequence of this process, however, was to restrict and threaten individual creativity. As capitalism, bureaucracy, rationality, and scientific thought strengthened, charisma became routine, religion was made irrational, and wonderment and interest in the world was smothered. If a degree of irrationality, chaos, and dynamism could be maintained under capitalism, then it might be possible to slow down or halt, if only temporarily, the diminution of individual creativity.

These structural views of society and social change - and the ambiguity surrounding the individual's place in all of this - were also characteristic of those who studied non-western societies. Firth (1951) seemed to have few doubts about the connection between culture and structure. Culture, he believed, was socially acquired behaviour. It formed the content of structure, and structure described:

> 'the set of relationships which make for firmness of expectation, for validation of past experience in terms of similar experiences in the future. Members of society look for a reliable guide to action, and the structure of society gives them this – through its family and kinship system, class relations, occupational distribution, and so on' (p.40).

Change was to be described by social organisation – by which he meant 'getting things done by planned action' or 'the systematic ordering of social relations by acts of choice and decision' (Firth, *op. cit.* p.36 and p.40). Put another way, social organisation was 'variations from what has happened in similar circumstances in the past' (*ibid.*). Structure, then, sets the precedent and provides a range of alternative possibilities, while social organisation 'is to be found the variation or change principle – by allowing evaluations of situation and the entry of individual choice ' (*ibid.*).

Twenty years earlier, Radcliffe-Brown (1930) had reached a similar view of structure. Stable society comprises networks of social relationships which necessarily form cohesive and integrated patterns, each part of that pattern (or structure) being dependent upon every other. Change is to be understood as the process of integration and disintegration. When this involves the disappearance of simple and narrow systems of integration (comprising only hundreds or a few thousands of people) and the emergence of more complex and wider systems (comprising millions of people), then social evolution may be understood to have taken place. But change is not always effective; nor, even if successful, does evolution necessarily avoid the problems that attend disintegration and ineffective re-integration. An insufficiently integrated society (a society in a state of *dysnomia*) suffers from moral unrest - a condition which manifests itself through, say, neuroses, revolutionary political movements, new religious sects (characterised by emotionalism and hysteria), forms of criminality, and increases in the rate of suicide.

For the Wilsons (1945), too, the movement of society from full integration - or, to use Radcliffe-Brown's term, a state of *eunomia* - to one of disequilibrium, produces circumstances in which people become unsure of their responses. Each person now begins to behave in their own way, such that their behaviour is, from the point of view of every other person, illegal, illogical, or unconventional: this is the root of social change.

By 1952 Radcliffe-Brown (who, in his previous writings, had often seemed to equate culture with structure) had come to view culture as little more than an abstraction, while the networks of social relationships - or structure - which connected human beings remained the centre of the social anthropologists' interests. Leach (1954), who shared these doubts about culture, was also uncertain about the reality of structure. He preferred to understand social systems as a model of reality:

'This model represents in effect the anthropologist's hypothesis about "how the social system works". The different parts of the model system therefore necessarily form a coherent whole - it is a system in equilibrium. But this does not imply that the social reality forms a coherent whole; on the contrary, the reality system is full of inconsistencies; and it is precisely these inconsistencies which can provide us with an understanding of social change...Every individual of a society, each in his own interest, endeavours to exploit the situation as he perceives it and in so doing the collectivity of individuals alters the structures of society itself' (p. 8).

Doubts over culture and structure, and, therefore, a return of emphasis on the role of the individual, had no place in Parsons' (1949, 1951, 1951 [with Shils], 1956) work. At about this time he was developing the view that the cohesion and stability of society could be explained by complex social structures capable of shaping and determining the actions of individuals. Indeed, the individual was merely the product of these forces. The presence of society, then, presupposed systems of structure and culture: a personality system (actors); a cultural system (wider values and status roles); and the physical system (the physical environment to which society must adjust). If a society was to survive it would have to develop specialist sub-systems or, in other words, certain functional prerequisites. The first sub-system he described as 'adaptation' to the physical environment in ways that allow the system to achieve its goals. The attempt to achieve these goals – that is, the mobilization of resources in order that certain objectives can be attained – constitutes the second sub-system. A society's economy and polity emerge from, and may be equated with, the 'adaptive' and 'goals attainment' systems respectively. Conformity to a shared system of 'value-oriented structures' or 'patterns' (the third sub-system), allows society to achieve a comparative level of stability. These values, Parsons argued, have their origins in cultural systems. But if they are to act as a stabilizing force – by justifying social roles, status, achievement, and ability – they must be institutionalised: actors must be socialised, primarily through education during infancy and childhood. The failure to socialise leads to deviance and prompts the intervention of the fourth sub-system – 'integration' or methods of coordination and control. Social change, in

Parsons' view, describes social evolution or, in other words, the splitting and re-integration of society into more complex forms. Central to this process is differentiation in both the structure and functions of these sub-systems and their constituent parts. Each alteration, each event of differentiation, has knock-on effects throughout each sub-system and system. The result is a constant process of splitting and integration.

The marginalisation of the individual is also characteristic of Foucault's vision of the world. Our historical constructs, he argued, emerge from the apparatus of power which manifest themselves in everything from intellectual discourse, architectural forms, and scientific reason, to administrative measures and legal statutes. Indeed, society comprises power which acts as a force directly upon the human being, transforming it into an 'individual', and providing it with a place in that society. It is from power, then, that the self emerges; it is power that objectifies the self; it is power that rewards and punishes. There are mechanisms through which individuals can, to a certain extent, liberate themselves from the power apparatus and thereby extract some happiness from life. But, for the most part, the individual is the effect of power and its vehicle (Foucault, 1980 p.46); and change amounts to little more than the substitution of one form of domination for another. To understand the evils of society we must understand the apparatus of power.

A similar tension exists in Bourdieu's (1980, 1990) view of society. He admits into his social world a role for the individual in maintaining and altering structure. Yet he also sees in this world, objective structures – structures which are independent of, and are capable of guiding and constraining, the behaviour and representations of individuals. These structures comprise relationships which determine the individual's access to social power or, in words, to social capital. This capital takes various forms: cultural (such as mastery of cultural practices), educational (such as formal qualifications), economic, and symbolic. Each form of capital may be converted into another. For instance, economic capital may be converted into educational capital and vice versa. Since capital (or social power) is distributed unevenly, there exists among the classes - each of which is characterized by the possession of certain forms of capital - a struggle to gather into their hands still larger quantities of those particular forms.

Between structure and capital, argues Bourdieu, lies *habitus*. This, in part, describes the process by which individuals are adapted to a specific social structure and imbued with expectations about the forms of capital to which they do or do not have access. *Habitus* also describes an acquired collective state of mind: 'principles which generate and organise practices and representations that can be objectively adapted...without presupposing a conscious aim at ends...Objectively "regulated" and "regular" without being in anyway the product of obedience to rules, they can be collectively orchestrated without being the product of the organised act of a conductor' (Bourdieu, 1980, p.53). *Habitus*, then, produces collectives whose sum is greater than their parts. To Bourdieu's mind, *habitus* transcends the distinction between individual and society.

The struggle for power and the patterns of power are reproduced through *habitus* and through the conversion of capital, especially into its symbolic form. Since it is merely an acknowledgement of, say, economic or cultural capital, symbolic capital works to reinforce and reproduce existing patterns of access to the various forms and concentrations of power.

In Bourdieu's world, there is some room for individual choice and decision, and the struggle for power and the patterns of power are not always reproduced faithfully. But for Bourdieu, like Foucault, human society is about the domination of one group of people over another; and it is about their domination by the structures which shape and drive them. At best, the lives of human beings, and changes in human society, are about the replacement of one form of control with another.

Derrida (1976, 1978) throws the burden of explanation on to the individual in a rather curious way. Society and its structures are, for Derrida, discourses: texts constitute the social world in a very real way. But texts mean only what we want them to mean: all is interpretation. Change, while partly about chance and contingency, is mainly about 'me'. 'I' become the arbiter of what the world is or should be. I have the authority to undermine, to overturn, or simply to ignore whatever I want in the world around me. Giddens (1992) attempts to find another, less radical, way out of thought centred around closed and determining systems of structures. In pre-modern societies, he argues, social life tends to be governed by 'external' influences stabilised as taken-for-granted phenomena (p.174). This contrasts with modern society in which there exist opportunities for individuals to exert some control over their own lives. A distinctive characteristic of today's world is the expansion of reflexivity – the incorporation of ideas about social life into frames of social action such that those ideas now begin to influence practice and transform social life. For instance, in his examination of sexuality, he argues that power imbalances between genders and the reflexive quality of modern institutions help to explain sexual commodification, sexual repression, and empty, compulsive and shame-ridden sexual lives.

'Sexuality became sequestered or privatised as part of the processes whereby motherhood was invented and became a basic component of the female domain. The sequestering of sexuality occurred largely as a result of social rather than psychological repression, and concerned two things above all: the confinement or denial of female sexual responsiveness and the generalised acceptance of male sexuality as unproblematic. These developments were reworkings of age-old divisions between the sexes, particularly the schism between pure and impure women, but they were recast in a new institutional format. The more sexuality became detached from reproduction, and integrated within an emerging reflexive project of self, the more this institutional system of repression came under tension' (Giddens *op. cit.* p.177-8).

The solution, in his view, lies not in social or political revolution. Reflexivity, constantly in motion, is helping to drive us towards both the ideal of pure relationships (relationships that are equal both emotionally and sexually) and further democratic reform (personal and political).

3.1 Social change, corruption, and thinking about corruption.

It is not difficult to appreciate, even from this brief and selective review, that a consideration of social change broadens our perspective of corruption in two ways.

(i) First, it gives definition to our earlier suggestion that corruption may be seen less as a 'phenomenon' and more as a name applied to many patterns and instances of behaviour, each of which is probably open to many interpretations. Thus we might view corruption as a manifestation of the confusion wrought by a clash of theological, metaphysical and scientific states of knowledge; or we might choose to look to aspects of social change which, as Bell (1976) suggests, emerge from the tensions between three realms of social relations – the cultural, the political and the technological-economic. Corruption might also be understood as an expression of uneven and uncertain shifts in society from a condition of compulsory cooperation to one of spontaneous cooperation. Durkheim's notion of moral de-regulation (which attends the rise of individual consciousness in a more complex society) may also be part of the story. Or perhaps we might view corruption as the froth generated along a line of transition, as tradition and emotion give way to rationality and bureaucracy? Alternatively, corruption might be described as a reaction to the threat which large bureaucracies (whether socialist or capitalist) pose to individual creativity. Polanyi's view of transformation might offer a similar understanding of corruption. Modern society, he argued, is characterised by calculating individuals pursuing their own interests. By contrast, pre-modern society, ordered through reciprocity and redistribution, is largely devoid of self-interest and the instrumental treatment of social relationships. Might we not conclude, then, that many of the explanations of corruption found within the social sciences (the denizen of modern western societies ruled by the market) offer us little more than perverse characterisations of reciprocity and redistribution? Meanwhile, true corruption – the breakdown of social cohesion and the erosion of freedom – is allowed to set in as the status of economic activities is elevated to great heights, as economic interests are given the highest priority, and as economic decision-making is centralised. Or perhaps, in the light cast by notions of disequilibrium and *dysnomia*, we might view corruption either as an expression of a society in the throws of disintegration and re-integration, or as a failure of socialisation and methods of social control? Or is society - which, by definition, comprises domineering power structures - synonymous with corruption? If so, then is the solution to overthrow the existing order, or to become part of society and, through the reflexivity of modern life, direct it to more positive ends?

(ii) Secondly, our discussion of social change illustrates that - in addition to the concerns we raised earlier about the tension between culture and structure - there exists a more complex and profound dialectic between, on the one hand, culture and structure and, on the other hand, the individual. We noted at the very beginning of chapter 1 that definitions of corruption often carry the sense that one is putting the interests of self before the interests of a wider body; yet, as we have seen, it is fair to say that for a great many writers the individual has a limited role in our explanations of corruption. Set against ideas on social change, however, we must ask ourselves to broaden our vision. While some writers are of the view that the individual is dominated - or even created and destroyed - by structural and cultural forces, others suggest that the individual is most alienated and unhappy when those forces are at their weakest; and while some writers believe that structure and culture have a presence greater than sum of the individuals who gave rise to those phenomena, others take the view that such phenomena cannot be understood except as products of the actions of individuals. Do structures and cultures explain the qualities of our societies and our individual social lives, or must we look to our own individual actions? This dialectic between the individual and 'the whole' (the structures and cultures of society) is one to which most discussions in the social sciences must eventually return; and it forms but part of a still wider and truly ancient debate.[*]

Two questions

From these observations, two questions emerge. First, why has this dialectic between the whole and the individual been of so much interest to us, and why does it remain so? Secondly, why is it that, in particular, culture and structure, often in their hardened[†] forms, are given so much emphasis in the social sciences today? Thus, for example, much of the discussion on corruption or on, say, the economic success of the overseas Chinese, begins and ends with structural and cultural analyses. Whether we are interested in the Chinese company, Chinese economic success, the political economy of the Philippines, or corruption, the presence and operation of cultures and structures (in which there is often little room for the individual) is so often taken as a given. We can also see this in, say, explanations of change offered by institutional economists. For North (1990), divergence in the paths of historical change is a central puzzle in the study of human society: in what ways and to what extent have societies diverged? And what accounts for widely disparate performance characteristics? The answer, believes North, lies in the differences and interactions between institutions and organisations. Institutions are defined as any form of constraint that humans devise to guide and shape human interaction, reduce uncertainties, and bring structure to everyday life. Institutions can be formal (as in the case of rules) or informal (as in the case of social conventions). The specific and prime source of social, political and economic institutions, argues North, are transaction costs: the cost of measuring the valuable attributes of the items being exchanged; and the

---

[*] See Hodder, 2002, chapter 4.
[†] By 'hard' I mean either reified, or treated as relatively objective phenomena, though with some role for the individual either desired or admitted.

cost of protecting rights and policing and enforcing agreements (North, *op. cit.* p.27). Informal institutions (these are socially transmitted and rooted in culture) give way to formal institutions as the system of exchange (and therefore transaction costs) becomes more complex. Like institutions, organisations (such as political, economic, social and educational bodies), bring structure and greater predictability; but they are consequences of the institutional framework. There are, North believes (p.4), perfect analogies to be drawn between institutions and the rules that define the game, and between organisations and the teams which play the game. In short, institutions determine the opportunities in society; organisations are created to take advantage of these opportunities. Change emerges from the interaction of institutions and organisations. As organisations evolve to deal with the game, they alter the underlying institutional framework. There is, in this institutional account, a sense of a role for human beings in that they set and re-set the rules by which the game is played. Yet they set the rules and re-set the rules according to a logic which is either buried deep within them or present in outside world: ultimately, human beings are shaped by their 'problem-solving software' (North, *op. cit.* p.25), by culture, or by economic logic.

In chapter 4 we shall consider answers to these two questions - why is the dialectic between the whole and the individual of so much interest to us? and why do these concepts, especially those of structure and culture in their hardened forms, seem to be characteristic of the social sciences today? The answers to both questions have significant implications for how we think about corruption and, indeed, about the social world in general. But for the moment we shall consider the immediate influence which this hardening of our ideas has upon the way we think about society and its problems.

(a) The hardening of our ideas narrows, gives substance to, and seems to clarify both the problems which we believe confront us and our analyses of those problems. This may be convenient, but we risk abstracting our subjects from their wider organic context and limiting their dimensions.

(b) It may also lead to a proliferation and fragmentation of phenomena. For instance, once it is transformed into a specific and hard phenomenon, 'corruption' must be split into numerous categories and sub-categories in an attempt to accommodate the dimensionality of the multiple actions and circumstances to which we attach the name 'corruption'. Another example is 'culture' and 'structure': as they harden, the one must precipitate out of the other; it becomes less easy to see them as synonymous or as mutually dependent phenomena; and certainly it becomes quite possible to focus attention *either* on culture *or* on structure, as if the one can be understood without the other. A further example is provided by changing definitions of structure. We noted earlier that structure is often equated with social relationships. This is certainly true of the writings of social anthropologists from the middle of the 20th century. Yet it is perhaps more common today, at least in some quarters of the social sciences, to understand structure as the institutional connections (the shared ideas and representations) which shape or define our expectations about our behaviour. Individuals (whose behaviour is moulded by the social structures they carry) are bound to reproduce those structures. Only to the extent that individuals are permitted by structure any discretion, is there any variation in reproduction. There is in this understanding the implication that social structures *also* comprise social relationships which may or may not always abide by structural conditions or expectations. Indeed, viewed through some of the more radical perspectives outlined above, the social world is mainly, perhaps exclusively, about the structures which govern human beings and their relationships. It seems that as our notions of structure harden, even our social relationships are squeezed out, such that structure becomes an increasingly refined phenomenon.

(c) With the fragmentation of phenomena comes a fragmentation of specialisms. Thus, for example, the structural-cultural context of Imperial China comprises quite specific - and often uniquely - 'Chinese' structural and cultural features, ranging from, say, Confucianism to the striking Christallean mechanisms of Chinese marketplaces, and from China's bureaucratic feudalism to the patterns of Chinese history. It is also to these features that we must look if we are to understand the economic success of the overseas Chinese in Southeast Asia, though in this case analysis is complicated by the need to take into account the structural and cultural features of globalisation and Southeast Asian societies. The adoption of particular interests and perspectives is to be welcomed; but the hardening and, therefore, fragmentation of phenomena and specialisms may become confused with the professionalisation of analysis. One consequence of this is that the development and discussion of ideas is restricted by the conviction that there exist social phenomena whose nature is such that only those people schooled in the mechanisms and peculiarities of those phenomena, and in the methods of their study, are able and qualified to understand them. The sense that ideas are important in themselves is gradually lost. It is now just as important for writers: to demonstrate membership of particular factions through their acceptance of particular ideas; and to demonstrate acceptance of those ideas through correct practice, method, and language. Another consequence (and one that is as curious as it is interesting) is this: if we accept reflexivity - the view that life imitates art - then scholars through their writing and their lectures may help to create problems that did not exist prior to their imaginings. In other words, representations of imagined phenomena are drawn into subsequent thought such that individuals begin to behave as if those phenomena exist in fact. Or it may be that the scholars' 'take' on certain problems exaggerates those problems in the minds of others whose behaviour is, as a consequence, also exaggerated. For example, it might be argued that patrimonial analyses of the Philippines and its endemic corruption, together with cultural-structural explanations of the economic success of the Chinese in the Philippines, may reinforce highly critical street representations of the political economy, inflate Chinese economic significance, and thereby discourage probity and erode confidence (Hodder, 2006).

(d) It should be emphasised that much of what we have said about the hardening of culture and structure we can also say about the hardening of the individual. As we transform the individual into an absolute, we must ask ourselves what *is* the individual? How did that individual come to be? How do individuals achieve cohesion, stability and coherence in their everyday lives? And how, with time and across the generations, are institutions and ways of life are sustained and altered? If we do not accept that the individual is moulded by structure and culture, and if religion is no longer an option, then we are led to explanations framed around psychological, biological, neurological and evolutionary mechanisms. To harden culture, structure, and the individual, is to create phenomena which have to be explained by reference to other objective phenomena and processes.

One response to these comments [(a) - (d)], is that the hardening of these ideas, reflects a truth about the social world. Culture, structure, and the individual, *are* abstractions; but they may *also* be converted into objective and autonomous phenomena; and although their states and the relative importance of these states is always shifting, they are, in both their abstract and autonomous states, central to an understanding of human societies. Our debates - centred on methodological holism versus methodological individualism, structure versus agency, or objectivity versus subjectivity - are merely indicative of our attempts to reconcile what appears to be, in the early stages of our knowledge, a real contradiction in the social world.

Yet this may be to go too far. We may treat our ideas as absolute, and we may behave accordingly; but this does not make them absolute. If we view ideas about self and world - such as culture, structure and individual - as representations, then the questions which now confront our attempts to understand the social world are of a rather different order. The *immediate* problem is to understand the dialectic between representation and practice. The *fundamental* problem is to understand the nature of thought itself. Since we do not understand thought, then one possible conclusion we might reach is that our representations - such as culture, structure, individual, god, or evolution - are formed precisely because we have no understanding of thought and our behaviour. In this case, how do we even begin to comprehend thought?

4.0 Conclusions

So how should we think about corruption, and what is our explanation of corruption? Let us put the comments expressed in the final paragraph of section 3.0 to one side for the moment, and ask whether we should accept that the many immediate and specific causes of corruption are best explained with reference to a dialectic between culture and structure? It is, perhaps, tempting to answer yes. But if we do, we must ask whether we are confining ourselves to a circular argument from which there is no way out. Should we, then, broaden our perspective to embrace an organic social world and a more substantial role for the individual? And should we accept that corruption - like culture, structure, and individual - may take on both abstract and objective forms comprising aspects of many ideas and practices with many dimensional antecedents? If we take this view, then we should indeed expect multiple explanations for these dimensional phenomena, some of which we have touched on in this chapter.

We might also expect to find within this dimensional organism that we call society - if it is truly organic in nature - universal principles at work. And certainly, winding its way through these multiple explanations, there does appear to be a common thread: a discordance between sets of practices, values and beliefs each of which are regarded by those who hold them to be acceptable and proper. The main fault line seems to run between those who govern and those who are governed. It is along this fault-line, on the fringes of government, that corruption is most prevalent; though fractures may run through to the heart of government. This fault line is most apparent when the government is alien or dominated by groups defined by ethnicity, kinship, education, language or some other kernel of association. Other fault lines, however, are created as a sense of what is or is not proper, acceptable, and important, alters; and these may cut across divisions among government and citizen.

It is MacMullan (1961, p.9) who describes this fissure in colonial West Africa most vividly:

> 'as an example of literate government operating in an illiterate society and how it differs from the same situation in an almost wholly literate society..., consider the confrontation of a police constable and farmer. The farmer is barefoot, and the policeman is wearing a pair of large, shiny boots, and this difference may stand as a symbol of their relative abilities to protect themselves in modern West Africa. The police constable is literate, he has learnt (at some pain perhaps) not only to adapt himself to a specific set of rules and regulations, but to wield them against others; he is an authority on the law, at least at his own level; he can arrest the farmer, or report him, and he has, again at his own level, innumerable official and semi-official contacts with officers of other branches of the government service. The farmer...is uncertain of the exact contents of the various laws that affect him, and uncertain how he stands in relation to them. He knows he should have a license for his shotgun but cannot be sure that the one he has is still valid or if the clerk who issued it cheated him with a worthless piece of paper. He knows he should have paid his taxes, but he has lost his receipt, and anyway there is something called a tax year, different from a calendar year, which "they" keep on changing, so perhaps he should have paid some more anyway. Even if he feels sure that he has committed no crime, he cannot defend himself against the policeman. To complain to the constable's superior would not be much good in the face of the *esprit de corps* of the police. He can defend himself only by going to some other member of the literate class, a letter writer perhaps, or if the case is really serious, a lawyer, but has none of the skills necessary to choose a competent practitioner, and he may be so misunderstood that his real case is never put. Even if he has a good case and wins, it may not do him much good. All the policeman's colleagues will know about it and sooner or later, of course, he *will* break the law. Much better to give the policeman what he is asking for, or if he is not asking for anything, better give him something anyway so that when something does go

wrong, he will be more likely to be nice about it. *A man does not*, says the Ashanti proverb, *rub bottoms with a porcupine.*'

This rift may also be described by the terms formal and informal. This is not, we have suggested, a division between the western and non-western. To regularise, formalise and, therefore, to make predictable what we regard as proper and acceptable, is a practical necessity. It is equally understandable why practices and ideas which invade and threaten what has already been regularised should be seen as uncertain, unpredictable, networked, fluid, and informal. In other words, informality describes not an alternative state to formality, but the active substitution of one set of regularised practices and ideas with another. Thus, a society may be portrayed as personalistic and informal not because it is less formalised, but because it is in this state of transition.

A possible conclusion which we might reach is that corruption is to be found at the boundary between attempts to regularise and make predictable conflicting ideas of what we believe should be. It is thrown up with the foam of social change. But does this mean that corruption is defined by what is or what is not found to be acceptable in any particular society? Do we apply the term corruption to what threatens and seems to undermine the current regularised patterns of behaviour and understandings of propriety? Is the presence or absence of corruption simply a matter of preference?

CHAPTER 4

The Causes of Corruption:
morality and attitude

1.0 Introduction

We have suggested that corruption emerges at the junction between discordant sets of values and practices, each of which is regarded by those who hold them to be acceptable and proper. We have suggested further that we tend to regularise and make predictable (or, in other words, formalise) what we regard as proper; while values and practices which we may regard as improper we characterise as uncertain, unpredictable and subversive (or, in other words, as informal). Corruption is in essence the friction generated at the frontiers of social change.

But is this understanding not too broad? Corruption is now understood as behaviour and circumstances which we happen to find distasteful or undesirable as the world around us alters. For instance, in societies attempting to develop a market economy and a democratic polity, either the market or democracy or 'traditionalism' may (depending upon one's predilections) be seen as the cause of corruption. Are we to accept that corruption is merely what we feel it to be? Or is there something about corrupt acts which makes them corrupt irrespective of our preferences? If so, then is that 'something' the presence of absolute moral standards from which any deviation in behavior is described by the term corruption? Perhaps one example is the substitution of self-interest for civic virtues and social responsibility, such that fellow citizens come to be seen as instruments or obstacles in an intense competition for wealth and power (Williams 1999).

As this same author notes, however, a moralistic perspective has attracted very little attention from modern social scientists. And it is plain why an interest in a moral perspective should be so limited: it is a lightening rod for censure. It draws us into an ancient and extremely contentious debate in which we cannot but take, or appear to take, a position on the meaning of morality and thereby offend one or other section of our audience. If we regard morality as objective and absolute, then we will appear to be ethnocentric and judgemental. We will have shown ourselves unaware of, or unable or unwilling, to acknowledge that our own culturally conditioned view of the world limits our appreciation of morality's varied social, political and economic contexts; and we will be led inevitably to advocate remedies which amount to little more than a cheer for western standards of conduct. If, on the other hand, we declare morality to be relative, then it might be said that we have given license to every and any evil and left ourselves with very little else to say.

Faced with this dilemma, we might decide simply to lay the whole question to one side and attempt to separate the moral dimension from the question with which we prefer to deal. Khan (1998) for example, writes that corruption may be ugly and immoral, but 'drawing the line between "acceptable" types of accumulation and "unacceptable" types is never easy. The more interesting question is to distinguish between situations where corruption has impoverishing effects from those where corruption allows rapid growth...The economic (as opposed to moral) problem is not corruption *per se* but the political structures which generate growth-retarding corruption' (p.37-8). This neat side-step of moral question is understandable. Yet we must wonder whether it is desirable? The people in whom we are interested make judgements on the morality of the actions which they observe, or perform, or which affect them for good or ill. Surely this moral dimension cannot be separated from an understanding of how and why people behave as they do, or from interpretations of the effects of their behaviour on others? Moreover, we cannot assume (for reasons set out below) that the scholars' commentaries, and the people who are the subject of those commentaries, have no influence upon each other. If we set aside the moral dimension we may provide succour only to those who believe that the end justifies the means. Or we may taint as both corrupt and immoral actions which are quite proper. Take Khan's (*op. cit.*) view that 'corruption is often an integral part of the processes of accumulation and social compromise' (p.37). If we suspect that what is termed corrupt behaviour is part of this accumulation and compromise and that, in some instances, it is economically rational and possibly even moral, then why describe such behaviour as corrupt?

How, then, should we regard morality? Should we think of it as being evaluative? If so, do our moral judgements rest upon belief or emotion? Or is it that our judgements are indistinguishable from moral actions? That is, judgements are moral precisely because there is no link between, on the one hand, feeling or belief and, on the other hand, moral actions. If it were otherwise, then it would be possible to lay a claim to a moral disposition while acting in quite another way. Moral judgements, in other words, are commands which tell any moral person what to do regardless of competing evaluations. They can be neither described nor understood as part of the natural world, for this would make of them things in which we believe. But whilst they are not of the natural world, words such as 'good', 'bad', 'right', 'wrong' and 'value' do describe a property and, in this sense, they are objective and universal.

Or might it be that reason itself is enough to lead us to actions that are moral and binding on all rational beings? If so, then how does reason lead us to moral action? Is it an a priori conclusion or does that conclusion emerge from a consideration of circumstances? One suggestion is that moral action emerges with an increasingly complex state of consciousness as self meets opposition from other competing wills. Out of this conflict and compromise arises the realisation that self can never truly be fulfilled until it respects the will of others, and acknowledges the moral law that binds together and forbids us to manipulate one another. It is not certain that we will reach this state of consciousness envisaged by Hegel. Leaving home and the safety and familiarity of our parents' values and ways, and entering a competitive world, is not possible without some rejection of home. In some cases this rejection is so intense, and the rupture so deep, that the emerging adult is compelled to reject all authority, norms and customs for the rest of their lives. We might expand this idea a little further: from the moment we leave home until the moment we reach fulfilment, we exist, for a large part of our lives, in a state of alienation, in a world that seems part from us. This is the root of our immorality: even if we are lucky enough to escape this sorry state of perpetual rejection, we are always tempted to reject, to seek revenge, to manipulate those around us for our own advantage.

Perhaps it is this state of alienation which leads us to the view that my freedom (which makes me who I am) is being threatened by other people. Constantly, they attempt (or so I might feel) to impose on me social rules and moral values; to make me perform and to turn me into what I am not - an object. It is this – being owned and attempting to own others – that is immoral. Therefore, it is not only imperfect institutions that are immoral: just about all institutions are immoral. They are structures of power whose *raison d'etre* is to compel the individual to adopt behaviour, values, roles, and patterns of behaviour which are not their own. A similar vein runs through Marxist thought. Particular systems of morality are associated with particular economic orders which pass through various historical stages. Capitalism is one such stage; and since it transforms individuals into things and makes of them a means to an end, then, from the Marxist's perspective, capitalism is immoral.

If we are not persuaded by these accounts of morality then perhaps our motive for moral action can be found in sympathy – a state of mind in which we are free of our own personal interests and desires so that we may feel for others and begin to think how their problems and miseries can be alleviated. And because we feel a common sympathy we arrive at common solutions. This common sympathy and these common solutions are the root of our morality. Or perhaps we need understand morality only as those actions which bring happiness or, as Smith believed, avoid interference in trade, the pursuit of profit, and the unintended benefits brought by commerce? Or should we be content to accept that moral values are better understood as temporary and essentially facile rules that allow us to protect and pursue our separate interests, and leave it at that?

Or perhaps we have been mistaken in our attempts to associate morality with any natural phenomenon or belief or emotion, or with reason or sympathy or happiness. Perhaps each of us should be more concerned with what kind of person we are: for it is not from our own qualities that moral actions spring? If we are rational, argued Plato, then we are led by our rationality to adopt virtues, to avoid shame, and to seek honour. Moral actions cannot be defined in advance: they are what the virtuous person does in any particular circumstance.

What, then, is morality? Is it any or all of these things, or none of them? Clearly we have different understandings of immorality, and different beliefs about who is being manipulated and who is being manipulative. Some of us may, with a degree of hostility, view morality and the institutions of society (or certain kinds of society) as instrumental and oppressive, while others will see in that hostile interpretation of society the very alienation that tempts us to immoral actions. But there does seem to be a common theme running through these discussions: that morality concerns our relationships with each other; that it is, in other words, communal. So often it asks that we treat each other not as means, but as ends. This seems to be true whether we hold morality to be real or rooted in emotion, belief, reason or sympathy; whether it is looked on as a device useful those who wish to manipulate, control, own and objectify others; or whether it is viewed as an expression of our desire to eschew instrumental behaviour. Is it possible to make the case, then, that morality cannot be relative, and that corruption is synonymous with a breach of morality? It is to this question that we now turn through a consideration of what I have elsewhere (Hodder, 2006) termed an attitudinal perspective.

2.0 An attitudinal perspective

Of central importance to this perspective are the terms 'social representation' and 'attitude'. Both these terms have long been familiar in philosophy, sociology and other areas of scholarship; and, indeed, we alluded to both terms in our brief discussion on aspects of social theory in the previous chapter. Whilst there are similarities between the ways these terms are more normally used and their usage in the context of our attitudinal perspective, there are also differences. In order to make these differences apparent, it is perhaps helpful to the reader if we set out the more common meanings of these terms.

It is probably fair to say that within today's social sciences both terms are most often associated with the work of sociologists and social psychologists. For the sociologist the term 'representations' is used generally to refer to images and texts which, through their portrayal of objects and phenomena, influence practice and understanding such that those objects and phenomena are subsequently altered. Just as art imitates life, so life imitates art. The term '*social* representations' is most closely associated with social psychology, and especially with the work of Moscovici. In this branch of knowledge, social representations are commonly understood as a system of values, ideas and practices with a twofold function. The first is to establish consensual order among phenomena. The second is to provide a code for social exchange and thereby enable communication among members of a community (Moscovici, 1973). Social representations are also understood to be *produced* socially: that is, they are produced collectively and remain the property of groups. Indeed, argue Duveen and Lloyd (1993), they exist prior to the individual: they are internalised by individuals and used as a framework through which they may interpret the world and place themselves within a community. Put another way, social representations are the elaboration of social objects by a community for the purpose of behaving and communicating. The belief that individual thought exists in isolation and that the individual can be considered as the basic unit of analysis is, therefore, entirely misconceived.

A not uncommon point of view is that the study of representations should replace the study of attitudes. These are widely understood as orientations towards other people, situations, events, institutions and ideas. They are held to be indicative of underlying values and beliefs; and, therefore, it is thought that they predispose individuals to behave in fairly predictable ways. Primacy is given to representations for numerous reasons. First, the study of attitudes is, in effect, the study of representations, but one which attempts to reveal and emphasise differences among social representations held by individuals and groups. This is quite simply to misunderstand the truly collective and social nature of representations. Secondly, it is often the case that individuals do not hold or are not able to express clear and well-formed attitudes. Third, there is considerable doubt surrounding the assumptions that stated attitudes reflect underlying values or beliefs and that there exists a causal connexion between those attitudes and subsequent actions. The suggestion that attitudes can be inferred only from actual behaviour does not remove this doubt. Fourthly, all these problems are compounded by what are held to be cultural differences in the meaning of attitudes.

The genesis of social representations is understood with reference to two ideas: anchoring and objectification. Anchoring describes the reduction of strange ideas into familiar categories and images, and their positioning within existing systems of thought. And because representations are social, anchoring draws the individual into the cultural traditions of the group. The second concept, objectification, also works to make the unfamiliar more familiar, but in ways that are more 'active': it turns the unfamiliar into the very essence of reality, transforming abstractions into concrete experiences. In the modern world, objectification is most evident in the guise of science (Moscovici, 1984, 1982).

These ideas require us to acknowledge we study through the medium of representations. For instance, an insistence that psychology is a branch of the natural sciences, and that psychologists must conduct their research in a laboratory and follow its experimental protocols, betrays the influence of particular representations of the social and natural world current within the field of psychology. The notion of social representations also requires us to acknowledge that western social scientists, and their western subjects, are heavily influenced by a particular representation - individualism. In view of this, and given the reality that our representations are social, then in our studies we must sample communities rather than individuals. We are also required to undertake research on 'non-reactive' materials or, in other words, to build up an understanding of the representations carried by archive materials (such as books, magazines and newspapers). This is important partly because these representations are 'frozen' whereas the psychologists' subjects, once they know that they are being studied, will alter their responses; and partly because those who study, and those who are being studied, are influenced by these representations. For all these and other reasons, a variety of analytical and methodological techniques are advisable. Chief among them are, for some writers, participant observation and unstructured interviews, during which an attempt is made to elicit representations from subjects through negotiation and the introduction of contrasting representations.

2.1 Representation, attitude, and practice

There are, we have said, both similarities and differences between the meaning of the terms representations, social representations and attitudes outlined above, and their usage in this book. 'Representation' or 'social representation' (the terms are used interchangeably here) are understood to refer to constructs of self (or 'I' or the individual), of the wider world, and of self's place in the wider world. By the wider world (a term which we use interchangeably with community or collective) we mean the pattern of relationships within and beyond our immediate experience.

We have elsewhere suggested a tentative explanation for our representations. We argued that our original and visceral constructs of 'I' and community are reasoned conclusions which emerge gradually out of our interactions with the natural world and, most importantly, with each other. These constructs ('I' and 'community') are generated constantly by these interactions, and they are manifold. It is only with the emergence of awareness that these multiple constructs are reconciled.* With the awareness of thought comes the question 'what is aware?' Since thought cannot think, the answer is to treat 'I' as if it were separate from thought such that it is now as if 'I' is the thinker behind thought. A paradox is realised (that of the thought that thought can think); and the many 'I's can be reconciled. And because we are aware that our sense and constructs of 'I' are rooted in large part in our relationships, we understand not only that we participate in relationships, but that we are of those relationships: that is, our sense of being and our constructs of 'I' and 'community' emerged from, and continue to be sustained by (and are therefore dependent upon), our interactions and relationships with one another.

Whilst these representations of 'I' and 'community' enable us to organise particular instances, and to operate physically within the natural and social world, this

---

* Whilst we have elsewhere (Hodder, 2006) suggested an account of the emergence of our sense of 'I' (or, in other words, awareness), of more immediate interest here are the qualities which this sense of 'I' brings.

is not their only effect or stimulus. Because we are unable to think before thought (and because, as a consequence, we can understand neither the nature of thought nor how nor why we think), we are compelled to form casts or moulds (such as God, culture, society, structure, or evolution) such that we feel we can now explain why we think and do the things we do. It is for this reason, too, that we dream in our sleep and when awake. That is, we dream - we extrapolate, and we imagine a world and our place within it - because we do not understand thought.

There is another source, or stimulus, for our representations, and that is their transmission through the written word and through sounds, images, and movement. But whilst they may take on material substance in the form of pictures, texts, and recordings, they have no independent existence. They are brought to life only through interpretation. Since the contexts of each mind - comprising reconciled 'I's and constructs of world and self's place in that world - are varied, then the expression of representations and their interpretation is varied. Bound into our subsequent representations of self and world, these transmitted representations may have a profound influence, but rarely in ways that are predictable or knowable.

The term 'attitude' is used here to refer to quite specific representations. It refers to our relationships: to how I think of you and how I think I treat you, and how I think you think of me and how I think you think you treat me. Still more specifically, attitudes describe the extent to which we view and treat our relationships as 'affective' or 'personal'. By an affective attitude we mean that we think of our relationships *as if* absolute - *as if* important in their own right. By a personal attitude we mean the extent to which we think of relationships as instruments: either openly or covertly through their presentation as absolutes to which we appeal as we attempt to bend others to our own will.

Since our attitudes are representations, they share the same roots as all our representations. They emerge from our interactions with the natural and social worlds; from our need to function as physical beings in those worlds; from our inability to think before thought; and from other people as we pass them amongst ourselves. But we may also look to more specific origins: an awareness of community and an awareness and reconciliation of self.

The knowledge of our own sensations and states of mind, no matter how illusory we might think them to be, are nevertheless keenly felt. Given this intense knowledge, it is only reasonable that we should take a personal view and, as best we can, manipulate and translate our relationships to our own personal advantage. Yet, as we have said, we also have in our possession another understanding of our nature: that we are *of* community, If we are to sustain, in any coherent form, our very *sense* of being as well as our *constructs* of 'I' and 'community', then we cannot afford to alienate ourselves. We are, therefore, persuaded to treat our relationships *as if* absolute – *as if* 'you', 'I', 'we', 'they', what we think each other to be, and our behaviour towards each other, are important in their own right. By this treatment of our relationships *as if* absolute, we mean that our relationships are openly and publicly declared as absolute; but in practice, and silently, we admit to ourselves that this is not in fact the case. This masquerade is necessary for two reasons. First, if it were openly admitted that they were not absolute we would acknowledge their instrumental quality. In doing so, and in the manipulation of relationships for our own ends, we begin to alienate self. Self begins to unbind, leading us into a state of incoherence and unpredictability. We become unsure of, and begin to deny, our own individual sense of self, and come to view it as an illusion. Nothing matters: other people are transformed into material to be manipulated for our own illusory purposes; and we may behave as we wish. Community falls away, and the non-existence of the self is reinforced. Secondly, if we treat our relationships as pure absolutes, as incarnate objective phenomena, they take on an immediate yet brittle power. The importance of relationships is now imposed upon us, presented to us complete and factual, a quality over which we no longer have any choice. And since those phenomena and their qualities are no longer understood to emanate from us, we cannot discover them for ourselves nor therefore appreciate them intimately. At the same time, if 'I' is made an absolute, then I am driven by my sense of alienation to seek to affirm the absolute quality of my self through the only way I can - the manipulation of others for my own purpose. So, too, by making of community an absolute, we are compelled to deny self. Each of us must subject ourselves to others whose ambition is hidden behind the community's well being; and as our sense of alienation takes hold, we also begin to manipulate those around us.

If we are to admit both aspects of our notion of being, then, as we have said, we must treat 'I' and 'community' *as if* absolute. Seen through this attitude (which we describe as affective), the value of 'I' is made dependent upon all of us. In this implied compact we bring to our lives true strength, predictability, reliability and equality.

Finally, practice is used here to refer to the practice of our social relationships. Coloured by attitude and informed and commanded by representations, practice describes how we behave: how I act and move towards you, what I say or do not say to you, what I do and do not do for you. All behaviour comprises practice: if you buy a newspaper without talking to me or acknowledging me, if I spend my time locked in my study writing my book, if you set me to work in a factory sticking labels on bottles all day, if we agree to follow a fixed procedure for a new curriculum or a new government policy, then we are putting into practice something* of what we think about each other and of what we believe to be our place in sets of relationships within and beyond our immediate experience.

---

* The matter is complicated by a distinction to be made between immediate representations and their echoes (see section 3.0 [I] (iii) below).

2.2 The play

We have argued, in effect, that there exists a play between our attitudes to relationships, our representations, and the practice of relationships. Attitudes colour our representations, and both (attitudes and representations) inform or command our practice; and the practice of relationships in turn is both the root of our constructs of being (from which our attitudes emerge) and the material about which we form our subsequent representations of the social world and our place within it.

Let us assume, for the purpose of description, that our representations and relationships are coloured by attitudes in their purest and ideal form. We might then imagine that viewed through the personal, my ends are everything. Empathy and anticipation are limited, for I am interested in what others think, feel, and do, only in so far as they impinge upon, or are of use, to me. And since I can, in practice, achieve my ends only through my relationships and through those relationships within and beyond my immediate experience, then relationships are all that I wish to see. My social representations are those of my networks of relationships, of alliances - monitoring, blocking, and manoeuvring. I place myself at the centre of a world undifferentiated. It is undifferentiated because I need make no distinction between different aspects of my life. Institutions, values, beliefs, practices, laws, and conventions - and even the notion that a particular activity is economic, social, political, artistic, or scientific - are construed as mere images resting upon the substance of our relationships. Beyond the centre of my immediate relationships, lie distant combines of networks. As I contemplate the expansion of my will across these combines, I envisage the lowering of unyielding, unquestionable, and authoritarian certainties, subordinate only to me. Drawn upon to inform practice, these representations lead us into coalitions that are suspicious, tense, rivalries, and unstable. In this world, image is everything: even authoritarian certainties are subject to manipulation. Institutions, matted with intrigue, are made porous; laws and conventions, processes and procedures, are circumvented or dismissed at will. Monitoring, policing, and hierarchy, must now be strengthened; combines are made still more complex; the possibility of instability increases; and the need for authoritarianism is reinforced. As a consequence, our sense of alienation and nihilism continues to deepen.

Viewed through the affective, other people and my relationships with them are important in themselves. Empathy and anticipation are released, for what other people think, do, and feel, are of interest to me in their own right. And because this is so, then here, in my social representations, I am no longer the centre of the world. Other people and our relationships are, for their own sake, to be insulated from manipulation. Our relationships must differentiate, the functional distanced from the social, such that the different spheres of our lives are clearly demarcated. To that end, and in order to achieve stability, we must agree that whilst institutions, values, beliefs, processes, laws, procedures, conventions, and our differentiated spheres of life, are subject to debate and change, we will treat them at any one moment *as if* absolute, and to which all, including 'self' are subordinate. In our mind's eye we come together as networks of relationships and combines of networks that are less exclusive, more open, and which take on forms more sharply defined. Institutions, procedures, laws, processes, conventions, and the spheres of activity, come to be seen as discrete and differentiated, but flexible rather than rigid; and we are interested in their intrinsic qualities rather than in their appearance. There is less need for monitoring, policing and hierarchy. Institutions, now less tangled and less porous, are more focussed, flatter, and sleeker; and the capacity for ever-larger scales of combines is much increased.

3.0 Implications

These ideas hold various implications for (I) the quality of the social world (the subject of our studies); and for (II) how we study that world.

(I) (i) The social world is bound by a profound commonality which finds expression through our sense and constructs of being and their dependency upon our relationships, our attitudes, and the play. Difference, we might surmise, reflects only a dislocation of self in world. This may occur either as we move quickly from one particular concentration of relationships (about which we have built detailed representations) to another set of relationships (about which we have yet to form coherent and detailed constructs); or as we enter a state of alienation for some other reason. In either case, it is a shift towards the personal occasioned by our dislocation of self and our sense of alienation which colours our representations of difference.

(ii) The social world exhibits moments of crystallisation. Thorough our common and mutually adjusted representations (coloured by our attitudes) we bring some measure of predictability and regularity to practice. This regularity may come to seem almost palpable as we form well-defined groups and cliques, processes and procedures, rules and conventions. This sense of concreteness we enhance through the fashioning of the material world into our buildings (within which we practice) and into our technologies, manufactures and crafts (with which we record and transmit our representations).

(iii) Our social world comprises elements of continuity. We have argued that we are compelled to create representations precisely because we cannot think before thought: thought is representation; and representations, including our constructs of 'I', are conclusions which emerge as a result of our interaction with natural and social worlds. It follows that our thought must comprise two kinds. One kind cannot be distinguished from action: they are imperatives which command immediate action. We cannot know these immediate representations of self and world, for at the moment they are formed and command action they are transformed by those same actions. They become representations of the self who performed those actions. These echoes - these representations which emerge as a conclusion of the actions taken - are the second kind of representation. These are the representations that we know; they inform subsequent action (but do not constitute imperatives nor, therefore, do they allow us to predict action); and we transmit them to one another, through our words, images, sounds, movements and recordings.

We might surmise, then, that there are two kinds of history. One is the product of our immediate representations - the representations that we cannot know. In this objective history we have exercised no direct choice, if by choice we have in mind a thinker behind our thoughts - a thinker who judges whether or not to take this or that action. This objective history comprises latticed chains of effects set up through actions commanded by our immediate representations. It is a context of tangible actions which have had tangible effects on each of us. Yet being the product of our immediate representations, we can never be sure why the actions were taken nor can we fully comprehend their consequences.

Entwined around this objective history there is another form of history. We have argued that we exercise no choice because there is no thinker behind our thought who judges and decides. But we have also argued that it is through the realisation of a paradox - that of the *thought* that thought can think - that our many 'I's are reconciled. The representation of an 'I' who performed this or that action, emerges as a conclusion of the actions taken: thus it is *as if* 'I' has made a choice. This representation - the 'I' who has made a choice - is bound into subsequent thought. It may then inform subsequent action, or it may be integrated into those immediate representations which command action. (Indeed, were it not for this representation - the 'I' who chooses - there could be no masquerade, no apparent choice both to accept the conclusion that relationships should be considered as important in their own right, and to behave accordingly.) In this way, an increasingly layered and complex representation of 'I' evolves: that of the 'I' who has made many choices and done many things for many reasons and under many influences. This history, of past selves in past worlds, is the history that we know. It is these representations (the layered 'I's who choose for many reasons and under many influences) which, if spliced into our immediate representations, may become part of objective history, but in ways and to an extent that remain unknown to us. Thus our representation of historical continuity is only an echo of an objective history - an echo whose faithfulness we can never be sure of.

In short, our actions have direct effects which run from one moment to the next and from generation to generation: but these we can never really know or explain. Our knowledge cannot but comprise representations of what we think has happened and why. These representations may have an important bearing on subsequent events, though again we can never be sure in what ways or to what extent this is so.

(iv) The social world also comprises change and discontinuity. These qualities are rooted in the nature of our attitudes and representations.

(a) Although representations of individual and community (or whole) describe a false antithesis, we nevertheless have powerful sense of both self and of community which, we have argued, lead us to strike certain attitudes towards relationships and which propel us back and forth between a personal and an affective state of mind.

These shifts in attitude are, to some extent, innate or spontaneous. If we deny or make an absolute of self or community, we move into a world that is personalististic and takes a form that is either loose and factionalised or, as an attempt is made to bring order and direction, strongly authoritarian. Yet the more we manipulate others, the more we deny our constructs of being, and the more alienated we feel, then the more we desire a return to the affect. The personal and the affective, then, are not dichotomous. Rarely, if ever, we will be faced with people who are in their attitude purely affective or personal. Both attitudes are always present within each of us and among us all.

A second reason for attitudinal shift is essentially practical. That is, a shift towards the affective is both a practical necessity if stable and effective institutions are to be created and maintained. More accurately, the creation and operation of institutions stimulates shifts in attitude towards the affective and the performance of the masquerade - shifts which happen to throw up more effective organisations.

The working of the organisation and the need to instil direction and discipline will confront expectations associated with social relationships, irrespective of whether our attitudes to those relationships are strongly personal or affective. Distancing social relationships provides the space for those who make up the company to behave, and to be treated, in ways which outside the organisation appear to be offensive. The most obvious, if somewhat crude, expression of distancing is the exercise of authoritarianism and centralised control. The wishes of the leader - his own representations of the world - take on an absolute quality, such that relationships between superiors and subordinates appear to be set aside. But as the organisation grows, as its tasks multiply, and as its complexities intensify, authoritarianism is unable to handle the demand for increasingly complex decisions. Moreover, the distancing of relationships within the organisation is a denial of the nature and origins of our sense and representations of self and community. This denial, and the consequential sense of alienation, is felt even more keenly under an authoritarian regime which, at its most extreme, appears to obliterate social relationships altogether. We are prompted, therefore, to seek refuge in the idealisation of our social relationships outside the organisation; and, as we do so, to define a clearly social sphere of life. Creating this social sphere and bringing to it sharper definition requires the performance of the masquerade. Within the social sphere we behave towards 'I', 'you', 'we', and our relationships, as absolute (as important and interesting in their own right). This is necessarily paralleled by the treatment of the walls and frames of the organisation – its rules, regulations, procedures and patterns of behaviour – *as if* absolute. This parallel behaviour is necessary; for otherwise in admitting the social essence of our rules and roles we would have acknowledged that our social relationships are indeed instrumental in quality. In this case we would have breached the social sphere.

However, at the same time that we treat our relationships - and, implicitly, the rules, roles, and organisation - as absolute, we must also admit to ourselves silently: that they are not *in fact* absolute nor *in fact* distant or separate from the organisation; that our relationships are also the material of the organisation and of all other aspects of our life; and that our rules, roles and organisations are but expressions of the practice of social relationships. This treatment of social relationships and of the social sphere *as if* absolute, and thus the implicit admission of the social qualities of the professional sphere, is essential to the protection of the social sphere. If we do not make this admission then "I' is made an absolute; and we create within our minds other rigid phenomena - 'you', 'we', 'relationships', 'rules, 'roles' and 'organisation' - whose meaning, presence and influence, are not dependent upon our common (but implied) compact to treat such representations *as if* important and proper in their own right. It is to these pure absolutes - now set above us - those in authority, and those with ambition, appeal in order to justify, explain, persuade and demand. This elevation of our representations and relationships, their separation from us, and our appeal to these hollow absolutes, nurture a strengthening sense of alienation. Our reaction to this is, at first, to move towards instrumentalism. Now, as this beach of the professional and social spheres grows, we enter a downward spiral of deepening alienation and instrumentalism, until we are propelled by our sense of alienation back towards the affect.

We have said that admission of the social essence of professional life must be made silently. Were it to be made openly, were we explicitly to regard the frames and walls of the organisation as but an expression of social relationships, then once again the instrumentalism of our relationships would have been made plain; the mystique of rules, roles and organisations would have been destroyed; and the social sphere breached. Social relationships (though they are the true material of the worlds outside the social sphere) remain a shadow, their existence and core significance acknowledged but left unspoken.

(b) The crystallisation of our representations - those periods of regularity and predictability in practice brought through a synchronicity in our representations - is also only temporary. With time, as our representations begin to layer and attitudes shift, our representations of self, organisation and wider world alter. Moreover, whilst those people who constitute, say, a company or a family may come together regularly (though perhaps this might be truer of a company), they also break apart fairly regularly. In the case of the company, its members break away from each other and from the company's procedures, processes, rules, and place, if only for a few hours each day. In the case of the family, its members may be separated from its conventions for hours or months or years, and reunite only occasionally. Each member takes with them their representations of company, of family, and of their place within all that and the wider world; and always their representations are coloured by their shifting attitudes. In the time apart, each member is part of the play of other instances: and the attitudes and representations which they took with them are now layered with new experiences. With this layering of   representations within and outside the organisation, and with shifting attitudes, come changes in thought and behaviour. Each time the company or family crystallises again, the representations which enable that moment of crystallisation will have altered slightly. This time the family does not seem quite the same; or perhaps coordination and compliance within the company is not quite what it was. Eventually even the most fundamental rules, processes, conventions and patterns of behaviour which at one time may have been unchallenged and unchallengeable, will begin to lose their importance. From afar we might imagine these moments of crystallisation as sun-glitter, appearing and vanishing with the ocean's swell.

(v) Since change in the social world is inherent, and since this is rooted in the very nature of our representations and attitudes, then we can infer that the social world which exists *in fact* 'out there' is not a pattern in itself set apart from each or any one of us, but a fuzzy composite of relationships and ever-changing dimensional events. Such coherence and order as we bring to, or experience in, our own lives is thus a function, not of what is 'out there', but of what is in each of us. Through our commonality of reason and our practical everyday lives, we adjust our constructs and the place we imagine ourselves to have within the wider world (and we may attempt to persuade or compel others to do similarly) such that we can, in practice, achieve some kind of *modus vivendi*. There is, then, no distinguishable or explanatory pattern 'out there' beyond the particular, except for other particular instances. These particular instances are able to function in themselves, and collectively on a wider scale, because the practice of relationships is informed by representations of the immediate and wider world which, though not accurate, enable particular instances to achieve a working fit. We must therefore concentrate on attempts to understand the particular sets of relationships we come up against or participate in.

(II) The implications of our attitudinal perspective for how we study our social world are numerous. When viewed through our attitudinal perspective, the social world and its apparent categories begin to dissolve. We ask ourselves to move away from certain dichotomies of thought such as free-will versus determined behaviour, the individual versus the 'whole', culture versus structure, or the historical versus the a-historical. Spheres of action (such as economic, social, political, and bureaucratic) and other categories of phenomena (such as corruption, social change, marketing system, social network, business, family, culture or institution) also break down. We recognise that they are representations of our common substance which, if bound into thought, may influence subsequent practice; and that practice may influence our subsequent representations. Nor, then, do we need allow ourselves to be distracted by questions over whether our perceptions of the world are real or illusory. Our representations - our thoughts about the world - are real. That is, they provide us with constructs – thought not necessarily accurate ones – which sometimes influence practice and allow us to function in the world, and sometimes do not.

Our thinking, then, is no longer confined within one or other representation. We can step outside, say, culture, structure, individual, and community, within whose parameters we often tend to think, and view these categories as representations. This is not to dismiss such categories, but to suggest that their relevance may alter with attitude and from one particular instance to the next as they are drawn into practice. Moreover, whilst we can step outside particular categories, we have argued that we cannot but think in representations, nor can we free ourselves of the play of representations, attitude and practice. The products of our studies (the book, the article, and the lecture) are representations coloured by our attitudes, and by the practices we come up against or in which we participate. And just as the scholar may pick up representations from the street, so the scholars' subjects my borrow representations from the scholar. If bound into thought, the academic's representations may begin to influence subsequent practice on the street, while street representations may begin to influence practice in academia.

But if we cannot think except through representations, if we cannot stand outside the social world, and if the writer's representations are coloured by attitude and practice, then how do we put together representations that might be just a little more faithful to the social world?

(i) Part of the answer is to enter a constant cycle of dis-aggregation and reformulation. As we begin the cycle, we are guided by our initial representations of particular instances and the wider world. We now begin to tease out the attitudes, social relationships, and representations that comprise those particular instances. As we attempt to do so, and as we attempt to communicate our understandings, we cannot but re-formulate our representations at different levels. For instance, there are: representations of the play of attributes that comprise particular instances (such as the acts of corruption within a company or political institution); representations of the world beyond our immediate experience (such as the Philippine political economy); representations that are of a more abstract form (such as traditional-modern transformation); and there are still more abstract representations of the principles of the play of attributes. These representations, however, are not the end to which we are working. They are frozen expressions of what our understandings *were*; and because they are profoundly coloured by our own attitudes and relationships, we must serve them up as material for subsequent cycles. Our representations, then, are not intended to provide an accurate explanation and description of the social world beyond or even within our immediate experience. They are simply the medium through which we continuously develop our understandings of the particular. And the more occasions we have to understand *a* particular, the closer we may be able to move towards an understanding of *any* particular. Without knowledge of thought we will never manage to grasp the principles of the play. But with each cycle, as we come to appreciate the dimensionality of particular instances, we might begin to form a sense of the simple commonalities that underlie the surface complexities and differences of the social world; and therein glimpse something of the principles of the play.

(ii) It follows that when faced with particular instances, our intention is to elicit the attitudes, representations, and a sense of the meaning and practice of the relationships of those who comprise those instances. At the heart of this - no matter how many people we talk to, and no matter how many different points of views of the same event we are able to garner – lies empathy. In our everyday relationships, even in the most transitory interactions, we have little choice but to attempt to establish a sense of what others are doing and thinking. Indeed, if a specific definition of relationships* is emerging from these pages, it is that they are abstractions - constructs of what you and I think and feel about each other. Empathy is also strongly implicit in our language -in what we write and say to each other. It is, therefore, essential in our studies, and this is so whichever approach we adopt. If I believe that you are shaped by cultural or global structures, then (whether or not you also believe it) I am assuming that I have a sense of your experience of the world. If I say that you are authoritarian in the way you run your company because you have been inculcated with Confucian ideals, or if you tell me this is the case and I say that I understand, then I am implying that I have a sense both of how you see and think about the world, and of your motivations, desires, and emotions. If I argue that, driven by global capitalism, you have centred your company on the family in order to keep costs low, I am again implying that I can see into your mind and through your eyes.

The question is not whether we are empathetic, but whether in our studies that empathy is hidden or open. To downgrade or deny empathy is to say that you and I are separate and can be understood only by reference to knowledge of the working of what it is - perhaps culture, structure, history, or evolutionary psychology - that shapes or conditions. It is to reify my representations, to claim that you can be understood only with reference to my representations, and to give my thoughts a status they do not deserve. Should we on the other hand admit empathy, then it may be that we can enter with immediacy an understanding of each other. With the central importance of empathy admitted we can now begin to reach more deeply into ourselves in order to understand one another. The representations we create are still only representations. They are not a claim to truth. What we are doing, and what we must allow ourselves to admit, is taking part in a collective enterprise. The representations of each of us, if subsequently

---

* See definition of attitude p.100.

built into the thoughts of others, may, for a short time, become part of their understanding of the social world and its truths. Whether the ideas, interpretations, and stories we create, will ever amount to more than this is the concern of hubris.

(iii) Our attitudinal perspective moves the emphasis of our studies in a number of other ways. First, our interest moves from general representations of the world beyond our immediate experience, to the particular and the non-conformist. The particular instance of social relationships, and deviations from what is expected, now become highly significant. The particular is no longer treated only as material with which to build up or confirm our vision of the general; nor do we treat deviations as being of marginal or occasional interest, either to be ignored or taken as a signal to adjust the general. Indeed, the particular and deviant *are* the social world; while the general - because it is but a representation that informs practice - has now become a means to help us understand the particular and deviant.

Secondly, emphasis moves to the street. So intimately are our ideas bound up with what we study, that we must attempt not only to dis-aggregate the world, but to do so in the field. It is only when faced with the complexity of the flesh, that we are likely to appreciate just how deeply and in what ways practice, representations, and attitudes, permeate each other. Only then may we begin to see just how far our representations, attitudes, and relationships, have led us to misread those in whom we are interested, and to remain blind to so many of their dimensions. As we move from the pages we read and into the street, possibilities and dimensions more complex than we could imagine now appear. Always we find departures from what we expected. And while we talk, listen, read, and act, and as we come up against the relationships in which we are interested, we find that what we study changes us, and that, in some small way, we change what we study. Thus we are compelled to revise our representations; thus are we brought to the beginning of a new cycle.

Thirdly, emphasis now moves towards more improvisatory thought. For now that we are less confined by our representational categories, now that emphasis has shifted to the street and the particular, and now that empathy and the intimacy between our study and what we study are admitted, we can be even less sure of the direction in which our thinking will take us. We should, therefore, be prepared to experiment with lines of thought, with styles and mediums of expression, even if they may at first sight seem a little out of place or even contrary to what are often seen to be the ideals of social science. We must reach across discipline and geography and many other aspects of human interests and forms of expression - art and literature, music and religion, philosophy and natural science. In other words, we may wish to consider broadening very dramatically our understanding of the legitimate subject matter of social science, and of the ways in which we communicate our ideas. Thus emphasis moves from a determination to set the channel and the tradition within which a study will be conducted, to a willingness to allow the unplanned emergence of understanding and lines of thought.

Fourthly, our interest moves from the frozen page to what is alive in the mind. Since we do not understand thought and are uncertain of our representations, we must pass through cycles of disaggregation and reformulation again and again. Our aim in this is not to construct such representations as we are able in order to freeze them on paper and present them completed and with a claim of accuracy. Rather, it is to excite in the mind of author and reader still more complex, fluid, and dimensional, representations of the play of attributes. It is in this - in what is alive in the mind - that the greater truth might be found.

3.1 Morality

(i) A further implication of this perspective is the moral dimension that it introduces into analysis. We have argued that relationships are the root of our sense and constructs of being. Morality (the principles concerning the distinction between right and wrong behaviour) is, therefore, concerned fundamentally with the sustenance of our relationships and the prevention of alienation. Morality defines itself as such because without those relationships (from which our sense and constructs of being emerge) there can be no *sense* of morality (no matter how we might subsequently codify morality).

(ii) Virtuous actions, then, are actions which preserve our sense and constructs of being; they are, therefore, acts which amount to the treatment of relationships *as if* absolute. Our representations of these acts – or in other words our virtues - must also be treated as if absolute. If it were openly admitted that our virtues are not absolute they would lose all force. If they were treated as pure absolutes they would, at best, be transformed into instruments for those in authority. At worst - now that they are presented to us complete and factual, now that we can no longer choose nor discover them for ourselves nor appreciate intimately their meaning and importance, and now that empathy and imagination are erased by the certainty of actions which these dictates compel us to perform - we find ourselves slaves to orthopraxy, living lives emptied of compassion, tolerance and consideration.

(iii) Our virtues, then, must emanate from each of us. They must be strained through an affective attitude which, if it is affective, is struck voluntarily and is not insisted upon. Since virtuous acts, if they are virtuous, must emanate from each of us and cannot be imposed, then they cannot be specified in advance. Since they cannot be specified in advance there can be no rule book to tell those of us who would be virtuous what we must do, nor be there any list of virtues. For instance, I could not claim to be virtuous if, merely to satisfy my own sense of virtue, I adhered to the command 'thou shalt not kill' and, by doing so, sacrificed an innocent life at the hands of a religious zealot. Nor would I be virtuous if, to satisfy my own sense of virtue, I prolonged the suffering of another person whose tortured physical suffering day and night without hope of sleep could be relieved only by death. Morality would have been turned into an absolute. I would have made you and your suffering an instrument of my virtue.

(iv) Since virtues are not absolute and since the affective cannot be insisted upon if it is to be affective, then we must also admit the possibility that there may be circumstances in which it is virtuous to strike a personal attitude to relationships if we are preserve our sense and constructs of being. Indeed, we have argued that if we are to know and to appreciate intimately our relationships and their importance, then we must choose to adopt an affective attitude and discover this truth for ourselves. We cannot, therefore, know and appreciate the truth without having moved from a state of personal and, as we have defined it, immorality. Without self-centred manipulation and without immorality, we can never know virtue.

(v) Although there is no list of virtues or compendium of rules to guide us or to compel us, we can nevertheless make the case that virtue must be common: a virtuous act performed in the circumstances in which we find ourselves would, in those same circumstances, be understood as virtuous by any virtuous person. Virtue must be common for if it were not we could not establish and sustain relationships with each other. If I begin to insist that morality is relative, and that my morality is particular to me, or if I declare particular virtues or my understanding of morality here and now in these circumstances to be universal, then I have begun to exclude and raise barriers to the world. My relationships begin to crumble and 'I' – which emerged from, and is sustained by, my relationships with the world – begins to unbind, creating in me a state of alienation, incoherence, unpredictability and instrumentalism. If we believe virtues to be relative to the group – family, friends, faction, clique, minority, or nation – or if we believe the virtues of the group to be universal, then we are not saved by our relationships within the group. Our virtues have become symbols of identity - we hold to what others do not. They are transformed into dictates - into inflexible, one-dimensional and uncompromising abstractions. Relationships outside the group are limited, while relationships within the group - now mediated through, and conditioned by, those abstractions which comprise identity - become increasingly indirect and are made into useful material for those with authority and ambition. We are led into a state of alienation: self unbinds, and unpredictability and doubt grows. In reaction, as we attempt to hold 'I' and 'us' together, we harden further our identity – those unique virtues to which we adhere but others do not - and succeed only in deepening our sense of alienation.

4.0 Morality and corruption

We have, so far, argued that virtuous acts are those acts which, in particular circumstances, are such that we treat relationships *as if* absolute. We also hold that there is no list of virtues; nor - save the advice that we should treat our relationships *as if* absolute - is there any compendium of rules which, if followed, make our actions virtuous. We understand morality in this way because without a willingness to treat our relationships *as if* absolute, our sense and constructs of self and community begin to unbind, and we begin to lose what it is that allows us possession of a sense of right and wrong, good and bad, however we might subsequently define these qualities. Even so, the advice that we treat our relationships *as if* absolute cannot be imposed. To do so would transform attitude and practice into instruments and destroy the quality of the affective. It would remove from us the *choice* to move from the instrumental and immoral to the affective. It would therefore remove from us a true and intimate appreciation of the meaning and importance of relationships. In short, without immorality and self-centred manipulation, we can never know virtue.

We might argue, then, that immorality describes corruption and that corruption describes immorality. Two questions immediately arise from this understanding of morality and corruption. First, if institutions commonly described as formal[*] are,

---

[*] Here we again use the term 'formal' in its more usual sense: relatively clear definitions - and, in practice, a careful observation - of spheres of activity (such as economic, social, political, and

as it is often said, 'de-personalised' or 'impersonal' and exist in a sphere quite separate from our private social relationships, then surely the understanding of morality which we have outlined can tell us very little about those institutions, and of their corruption tells us only that the social and the institutional have become blurred? Secondly, if corruption describes immorality, and if we understand corruption as a move towards the personal, then must we not conclude that societies in which the personal is strong are fundamentally immoral, and that societies in which the personal is weaker have the greater share of morality? Furthermore, if we accept that corruption amounts to a blurring of the social and institutional, then are we not saying that formalised societies are the more virtuous? Let us deal with these two questions, and then set out important riders to our answer.

(i) First, what does our understanding of morality tell us about institutions? We have argued that the treatment of relationships *as if* absolute enables us to establish and sustain: our relationships; a sense of 'I' and community; and reasonably coherent representations. We have further argued that our relationships are neither separated from, nor embedded in, nor have in them embedded, even the most de-personalised and de-humanised of institutions. Our institutions *are* our relationships. The shifts in the qualities of institutions (which are usually described as, say, formal and informal, or impersonal and personal) are expressions of shifts in attitudes to our relationships. We may now add another dimension to our understanding of corruption and immorality. We understand corruption as a move away from the affective. This is partly because without the affective we begin to lose our sense of what we are and our sense of right and wrong; and partly because it is to move away from an attitude which (through the

---

bureaucratic) and of the rules, laws, roles, duties, conventions, procedures and processes which make up institutions, their boundaries, and their interactions. 'Informal', therefore, describes a blurring and confusion of spheres, roles and institutions, and a more haphazard, unpredictable, and selective application of rules, laws, procedures and processes. However, we have noted elsewhere in this book that it might be more helpful if 'formality' were used to refer to what is accepted and acceptable.

performance of the masquerade) will allow the effective working of our institutions while defending the social sphere and the integrity of our relationships.

(ii) In reply to the second question (is immortality and corruption rife in a society in which the personal is strong?), we might answer that it may be so, but it is not certain. By the same token, there is no certainty that a society in which the affect is prevalent has the greater share of morality and propriety.

It is by way of explanation of these latter statements that we are brought to two riders. These emerge in the light of our earlier arguments that the treatment of relationships *as if* absolute should not be imposed; that there is no list of virtues, or rules for the virtuous; and that we cannot appreciate morality and our relationships without knowledge of immorality and instrumentalism.

Our first rider is that the movement away from the affective does not necessarily amount to corruption or to immorality. There may be instances in which the treatment of relationships as instruments is neither corrupt nor immoral. This is so because such behaviour is, in those particular circumstances, necessary if we are to preserve the affect. Indeed, our second rider is this: given that we cannot truly appreciate morality without immorality nor truly understand the meaning of our relationships without instrumentalism, then we may say that the greater risk for descent into corruption and immorality is likely to come not from personalism but from what we might call Puritanism.

We have argued that where the affective is strong, *explicit* social life is limited to the social sphere (family and friends). Through the practice of our masquerade, the social sphere is defended (and an artistic and literary intensity emerges) while organisational life becomes more professional and effective. But now circumstances are created that may begin to work against the affect. As thought and practice become increasingly segmented and categorised, we are in danger of losing sight of the true social quality of economic, political, and bureaucratic spheres, and of the common sympathy between thoughts on what we come to regard as different areas of knowledge (such as artistic, scientific, emotional, intellectual, economic, political, anthropological, and geographical). In addition, the scale and complexity which the performance of our masquerade has allowed us to bring to organisations is such that, within an organisation, each member is separated from most other members. In these conditions we may come to believe that - in order to maintain predictability and precision, and therefore complexity and scale - we will need to treat our relationships and representations (and therefore our institutions, processes, procedures, rules and roles) as absolutes. We convince ourselves that our representations, which once aided us in the coordination of our relationships, have taken on their own independent and autonomous existence, and now direct our thoughts and actions. Stories, myths, theories, conspiracies, and interpretative devices, are treated increasingly as objective phenomena; and it is these 'hardened' representations that now inform our subsequent practice. Problems and fears, first manufactured within our minds, now take on distorted and more expansive form in the world around us; and a contradiction is now established. On the one hand, alienated by our own imaginings and fears, and with little stake in our dreamt non-social world of objective social phenomena, we desire to manipulate this world for our own advantage: we are tempted towards the personal. Yet, on the other hand, there is a desire to resist: the practical necessity of maintaining complexity and scale reinforces our sense of the importance of the affect, and seems to demand that we treat our rules, roles and institutions as absolute and that we do so with unselfish obedience. We feel ourselves compelled to seal the social sphere, and to treat with still greater vigour our relationships as pure and absolute. We have now begun to impose the affect upon ourselves and others; and, consequently, we must deny or suppress instrumentalism. With this Puritanism grows a disgust with any imperfection, any symptom of instrumentalism, in ourselves and in our rules, roles and institutions. Thus are we consumed gradually by an obsessive determination to eradicate the instrumental and imperfect, to impose orthopraxy and, unknowingly, to remove from much of our lives compassion, consideration and tolerance. In this frustration of the personal, in this outlawing of the instrumental, in this denial of what we are, in this intolerance of imperfection in ourselves and what we do, we run the risk of violent counteraction and sudden return to an intense and ruinous personalism.

We might suggest, then, that corruption (understood as a move towards the personal) is the route to morality. This is because the personal leaves us acutely sensitive to the social quality of institutions, procedures, processes, rules and roles; and we are still left with the choice to treat our relationships *as if* absolute. Puritanism, however, bars us from this route, temporarily at least. We forget where morality lies, and soon we forget to care that we have lost sight of it. Only when the repression of self and instrumentalism can no longer been sustained and, on a sudden, we begin our return (possibly violent) to the personal, do we remember why we should have cared all along.

5.0 Conclusions

In this chapter we have argued that each of us comprise highly complex dimensional representations; that these emerge from our sense of being and from the forms of our constructs of being (self and community); and that this sense and these constructs of being spring from, and are sustained by, our relationships. If we are to achieve a balance between self and community, and thus save ourselves from a descent into alienation, we must treat our relationships, and so our constructs of being, *as if* absolute. This attitude (which we have described as an affective state of mind) we achieve only temporarily: we are continually being drawn back and forth between the affective and the personal - a state of mind in which our relationships (and so our constructs of self and community) are treated as instruments, either explicitly or covertly in the form of absolutes to which we appeal in our attempts to manipulate others.

The move away from the affect and towards the personal is associated with a higher incidence of practices which may be regarded as immoral and corrupt. This shift in attitude is described as corrupt and immoral for two reasons. First, it leads us into a state of alienation in which self is unbound, our thought and practice becomes increasingly incoherent and unpredictable, and our sense of right and wrong begins to crumble. Secondly, it dissolves our masquerade such that the efficacy and flexibility of our organisations (or institutions) are compromised.

A number of qualifications attend this understanding of corruption and morality. Movements in attitude and practice are not peculiar to any particular society: they occur constantly within all societies at all times and within each of us. Shifts in attitude and practice away from the affect and towards the personal do not necessarily amount to corruption or immorality. And the affective may lead us into a state of mind in which we reify our relationships and representations (including those which we describe as institution and virtue), and deny instrumentality (and immorality), self, and the social quality of life outside the social sphere. In this, we attempt to deny what we are, and risk a violent and destructive reaction.

How, then, does this help us to *explain* corruption? What, if anything, can we say about the reasons for behaviour that might normally be understood as corrupt? We can suggest a number of explanations, but we must preface these with two qualifications. First, aside from the property that they do not sustain our relationships (and thus, for the reasons we have set out, lead us into a state of alienation and weaken our institutions) there can be no typology for, nor any compendium of, corrupt acts. The qualities of corruption and immorality are dependent upon context, but acts possessing those qualities would, in the same context, be understood as corrupt and immoral by any person with a sense of virtue. We can, then, provide explanations only for particular acts. Any general explanation must be limited to an explanation of shifts in attitude which make corrupt acts more likely (but not inevitable). Secondly, any such explanations are only representations and must form part of further study. In this, our explanations would be subject to rounds of dis-aggregation and reformulation as we attempt to unpick the play of representation, attitude and practice on the street and within scholarship. They are therefore subject to alteration or, perhaps, to radical change.

(i) Within each of us, attitudinal shift towards the personal may, to some extent, be spontaneous (see sections 2.1 and 3.0 above). A fortuitous, or unfortunate, concentration of people whose attitudes happen to be strongly personal may make instrumentalism more likely and the manipulation and distortion of rules, roles, processes and procedures more possible. As a result, members of the wider organisation, as well as those members who are already behaving in a corrupt manner, become increasingly alienated; instrumentalism becomes more pronounced; corrupt acts become more prevalent; and a state of alienation becomes still more extensive.

(ii) A second explanation is that stimuli for shifts to an affective attitude on any scale in one society may have emerged relatively late in comparison to other parts of the world, and have yet to work themselves through. These stimuli, we might imagine, are manifold and common. The intensification of trade (exchange for profit) and, by definition, unequal exchange - through its initial prompting of instrumentalism and a sense of alienation - may encourage the deepening of the affect and (as attempts are made to preserve the affective content of social relationships) the creation and sharpening of social sphere of life. A still more important stimulus may be the proliferation of businesses, especially those built around the family. Making an enterprise work requires a conscious effort to distance family relationships (and the friction and emotions they generate) from the day-to-day running and longer-term planning of the business. As the performance of the masquerade within the organisation and the deepening of the affect outside it take hold, attitudinal change and the strengthening of institutional life may be encouraged more widely. A further, and equally pragmatic, stimulus to attitudinal change may be found within the institutions of government. If they are to exist as more than brittle shells, authoritarian institutions and practices (which may have been created as a means of enforcing one set of strongly personalistic relationships over another) may stimulate the deepening of the affect and the performance of the masquerade; the political and practical necessity for more effective and professional institutions will add grist to the mill. Authoritarianism, then, may carry the seeds of its own transformation. Yet another stimulus may be the moral teachings of religious bodies at whose heart lie a belief in the truth and affective content of relationships with one another. Associations, particularly those with a religious and charitable bent, may also help to promulgate shifts in attitude through their external activities and as part and parcel of their need for stability and organisational strength. From these various hotspots (business, political and bureaucratic institutions, Church and association) as well as from the spontaneity of the human condition, shifts in attitude might begin to percolate more widely through society.

(iii) A third explanation may be the presence of dampeners on these stimuli to attitudinal change. Where personalism and a sense of alienation are strong, we would expect the presence of acutely negative representations - of a cold, disinterested, and exclusive world in which most people are out to further their own interests. These negative representations may take on considerable power and coherence through the mass media and, indeed, through increases in the sheer volume of academic publications. They become so prevalent that people, who have (up to now) remained honest, begin to feel (perhaps wrongly) that they are alone in their honesty and have little incentive to remain honest any longer. Meanwhile, those in positions of authority, and who are already working things to their own advantage, may feel uncomfortable to see around them others whose state of mind is less personalistic and more affective.

(iv) A fourth explanation may be the presence of circumstances which encourage shifts in attitude away from the affective and towards the personal. A strongly affective and complex society which is becoming Puritanical and in which, as a consequence, the repressed desire for a return to the personal is building, may constitute one such set of circumstances. Another gentler route from the affective to the personal may begin with the hardening of our representations. As the scale and complexity of organisations increases, there may be a temptation to deepen the social sphere (to the extent that we lose sight of the social quality of life outside that sphere) and to transform into absolutes our rules, roles, processes, procedures and other representations. But now these representations - which are even less able to cope with the dimensionality of the world, precisely because they are held to be fixed, accurate, and autonomous - begin to splinter into countless categories and sub-categories of phenomena. As a further consequence, as we become drawn further and further into our fragmenting specialisms, we create unifying dogmas without which we would not be able to communicate with each other. The hardening of our representations may also begin to reinforce, and may in turn be reinforced by, practice within academia. As our representations harden and fracture, it becomes easier to treat them as objects, possessions or trophies, and easier to think of them as instruments for personal advance. Ideas are transformed into bases of association - or kernels - around which relationships and cliques are formed, and through which influence is wielded and hierarchies maintained. And soon our ideas seem far less important to us than other kernels such as scope of conversation, vocabulary, speech, dress, or mutual friendships. In this personalistic atmosphere it is perhaps not surprising that scholars should begin to view the world around them as de-humanised, repressive, and hostile. In their mind's eye each of us tries to dominate the other; and all of us are dominated by cultures and structures in which relationships, transmuted into forms of capital, are embedded. As the academics' representations - transmitted through their students, their publications, and their pronouncements - begin to inform practice, their once-imagined fears take on substance.

*   *   *   *   *

The more immediate problem, however, is not to explain corruption, but to think about how we can begin to unpick the play of representations, attitudes and practices in particular instance in the field; and to begin to cycle and reformulate our representations of corruption, its causes, and its effects. To this question we shall now turn in our discussion on the solutions to corruption.

CHAPTER 5
Solutions

1.0 Introduction

It would seem only sensible that attempts to deal with behaviour regarded as corrupt should be informed by our explanation of corruption and our understanding of its effects. A structural or institutional view would demand adjustments to organisations, procedures, rules, laws and conventions (or, to use Nathan's [*op.cit.*] phrase, the patterns of incentives outside an actor's head). These might include, say, the introduction of monitorial procedures, better pay, and harsher sanctions. A softer, cultural view would look to propagate 'norms' (the internal incentives) that regulate behaviour and reinforce a sense of mutual trust and responsibility.

We noted earlier (in chapter 2) that structural explanations hold sway over the analysis of corruption. Understandably, then, many of the solutions proposed in the literature are concerned with institutional adjustments and innovations. This emphasis is further strengthened by political considerations: politicians, bureaucrats, and non-governmental agencies (domestic and international) often feel they must be doing something that is visible, immediate, concrete, and delivers 'value for money'. Consequently, whatever doubts we might entertain, and whatever alternatives might be preferred, it is institutional reform that is most commonly discussed and acted upon. It is, therefore, to these structural solutions that we turn first.

2.0 Institutional measures

(i) The scale of institutional and procedural adjustments often envisaged may be very grand indeed. This makes complete sense if it is believed that the cause of corruption is rooted in the broad structural features of society rather than in specific institutions or a particular set of institutions.

Perhaps the most radical solution envisaged, and it is one which is occasionally practised (as in the case of China and the former Soviet Union), is to remove the entire institutional framework of the polity (along with the politicians who inhabit it) and in its stead set up another political system thought to be less corrupting and staffed by politicians and bureaucrats who are thought to be more honest. Military rule is another possible option. Replacing politicians with an officer corps, argues Huntington (1970), may have a number of advantages. It de-politicises administration, reduces the political demands on it, and is therefore bound to eliminate certain expressions of corruption. The new military class - less wedded to social kernels (such as language, ethnicity, kinship and place of origin), less materialistic, and less driven by a desire for self-aggrandisement - is likely to be more cohesive and imbued with the mores of self-sacrifice. It is therefore more likely to professionalise the administration, provide for the nation a clear sense of direction and, in these senses, play a progressive and modernising role much like the protestant emperors of Europe (*ibid.*). Purges of a lower order often take the form of anti-corruption campaigns. These, too, seem to offer direct and immediate solutions and, by making examples of the guilty, may work to prevent further abuses of power.

An alternative and less radical solution - but one that is nevertheless grand in scale - lies in the hope that nascent, but positive, changes in society might be encouraged further. Patrimonial analysis suggests - in the case of the Philippines (as we noted earlier in chapter 2) - that the state in its personalistic, informal and irregular qualities lies some distance from a strong, regularized, formal, impartial, legal-rational economy and polity of the kind described by Weber as a bureaucratic administration. In particular, argues Hutchcroft, the Philippines lacks calculation in the administrative and legal sphere; and family and business are not clearly separated. The essential question facing the Philippines (and many other developing countries) is how it can free itself from the bonds of patrimonialism and transform itself into a regularized, legal-rational, and bureaucratic state? As Hutchcroft (1998) and Callaghy (1989) point out, no theory exists to account for transformation. But Hutchcroft, following Weber, suggests that change might come from two directions: from below, prompted by the balancing out of interest groups (as competition amongst them intensifies) and by the entirely pragmatic demands of private capital for predictability and the rule of law; and from above, through the introduction of selected reforms, especially of the government's relationship with business.

The advice which seems to run from this, is that it is better to support these interest groups than to confront them: go with the grain of society's evolution. Take, for example, Khan's (1998) argument (see chapter 2) that corruption in Asia (south, southeast and east) is the re-ordering of the patterns of wealth and rights and, as such, may hinder or promote economic growth. Strategies to deal with corruption will work *only* if they contribute to the processes already legitimising those new patterns. The identification of these processes does not lie within the scope of Khan's paper. But we do get a sense of those patterns which are thought to encourage growth in some of the countries in the region and which, presumably, ought to be legitimised: centralised power in South Korea and Malaysia; the merging of political and economic elites in Thailand; and, in all three, the diminution of an intermediate (non-capitalist) class, and flexibility in the re-allocation of rights as economic circumstances change.

Theobald (1990) broadens the analysis even further and suggests that solutions lie partly in what the West thinks about itself. Our concept of a modern and clean state is the product of capitalism at a particular time in its development; and, in practice, these states are not entirely clean. The legal-rational principles which emerged from capitalist industrialisation in the shape of formal institutions and structures (political, bureaucratic and economic) did not eliminate personalism nor confine it only to the private sphere. They were fashioned into a kind of steel net drawn tight at the bottom of the bureaucratic hierarchy and loosened at the top where distinctions between public and private spheres were far less clear. This fact was not considered to be a problem: the net surrounding the most visible areas of the state (routine administration) at the base of the hierarchy was strong enough to contain personalism, while the hierarchy's top was hidden from public view by the absence of social contacts with its base. It is the application of this model to the third world which generates many of the problems that we see there today. A modern state apparatus set upon economic and social foundations ill-suited to bear the edifice (the huge demands made upon a materially weak public sector, aggravated by pre-modern forms of exchange, have been especially crippling) made the practice of corruption on a wide scale inevitable.

Not only has the model failed to work in the third world, but it is no longer applicable in the West. Here the size and the scope of the state have declined, leaving outside respectable society a large and growing underclass among whom crime is habitual and often well organised. As we come to understand that once again states in the West need to grow in size if we are to solve this problem, then perhaps we will finally acknowledge that a similar response is also needed in the third world.

Theobald's critique of the West, and of the assumptions which we often hold about the West, is interesting in that the solutions proposed (increasing the size and scope of government) run directly against the more common view today that corruption is best dealt with by reducing the role of government and giving more rein to the free market. The connexions between lighter government and less corruption are thought to be numerous, and we have alluded to some of these already. Efficient and effective legal, political and bureaucratic rules and procedures are more likely to be produced if they evolve around businesses' natural demands for predictability and fairness; the pressure on politicians to be even-handed and accountable will grow as competing interest groups develop; and administratively-created scarcities and other opportunities and incentives for corruption will diminish as administrative functions, regulations, and civil service posts are shaved away.

(ii) Other writers and practitioners bring a little more precision to anticorruption efforts, arguing that these must comprise batteries of specific and often quite technical solutions. Institutional adjustments need not be less ambitious than wholesale systemic revolutions: indeed, they may be more sophisticated both politically and administratively.

(a) Perhaps the most important and fundamental adjustment, or so it is commonly thought, is to divide powers and responsibilities among the three main branches of government - the legislature, judiciary, and the executive (and its bureaucracy) - such that each is able to counterbalance and scrutinise the other. Within this arrangement, further divisions of powers and responsibilities, and a further layering of supervisory agencies and protocols, are thought to be important if the state is to be kept clean. Procedures are introduced to ensure that no one official is responsible for authorising, processing, recording and reviewing transactions. The official's section is examined by the section's department, and the department is monitored by the organisation. The organisation's activities are also cross-checked and overseen by other government institutions. And all of this is policed by, say, independent auditors, legislative oversight committees, and various anticorruption agencies and boards. Among the most important of such agencies, or so it is often thought, is an ombudsman empowered to investigate, bring to book and prosecute even the highest ranking officials and politicians, for it is their example that will have most influence on their subordinates.

A further, and perhaps the most important, overseer is created by ceding to those who are governed ultimate authority to remove from office those who govern them. In addition to the expansion of suffrage, other vital components of anticorruption strategies are thought to include: open government; well-informed citizens who participate directly in government's decisions and policy formulations; freedom of thought and expression; and the effective defence of these qualities. A free press is also thought to be essential, together with freedom of information statutes, mandatory disclosure requirements, and open-meeting laws that compel government agencies to submit themselves, their procedures, and their decisions to the citizenry's direct questioning and proposals for improvement. Part and parcel of this openness are limitations on the application of 'confidentiality' to documents. For example, income tax assessments and payments should be made public.

If these kinds of changes are to have teeth, then changes to legislation and to the penal code may be required. Insulating whistleblowers from demotion, reassignment, ostracism, or even violence and death, may be necessary if there is to be effective monitoring at any and every level. And underlying all of this must be efforts to improve the independence and professionalism of the judiciary.

(b) It would appear that corruption is best avoided or mitigated through the creation of various layers of oversight such that each official (and elected politician), each section, each department, each organisation, and each segment and branch of government, oversees the other and is liable to investigation and prosecution. If these kinds of arrangements are to work effectively, then it would seem to make sense that rules, roles, conventions and boundaries of authority are made clear to staff and that not too much scope for creative interpretation is allowed. In short, rules and procedures must be clear, simple and precise; greater specificity should be brought to lines of authority; and discretionary powers should be reduced.

However, a heavy reliance on a complex and tightly prescribed lattice of controls and supervision creates an atmosphere in which individuals, especially if they are honest and capable, will feel that they are not trusted. And if they should feel that no one believes in their honesty, and if their honesty is left unrecognised, then why should they remain honest and competent? Clearly, there have to be incentives to remain honest as well as disincentives to become corrupt. These incentives commonly include improvements in the pay - and in the length and certainty of employment - of competent and proficient bureaucrats. This works to raise the social and economic status of officials, strengthens confidence, fosters an *esprit de corps*, and gives them a deal to lose should they become corrupt.

(c) No matter how much pay and conditions of official are improved, the material and financial rewards offered by business are likely to be greater; and no monitoring system which allows a degree of trust, creativity, and personal development, is going to be completely effective. It is therefore important that, as far as possible, the public sector should be insulated from the private sector and its temptations. Here we are concerned with direct attempts to secure unfair advantage (such as bribing officials), and with more subtle and unspoken forms of influence (such as the exchange of favours and the cultivation of loyalties and affections). For instance, cultivating relationships with ministers partly in order to persuade them to gear education towards the provision of particular skills for certain businesses today, is unlikely to be in the best interests of wider society in the longer term. And if economic affairs should become too central to the thinking and actions of government, then officials might come to

136

believe that their prime function, and that of the rest of the populace, is to serve the interests of business.

Insulation may therefore take many forms. These might include: legislation to compel firms to submit themselves to tougher financial controls and more stringent and rigorous scrutiny by external accountants and auditors; criminalising the treatment of bribes as tax-deductible business expenses; the introduction of post-employment restrictions which prevent former government officials from making personal gains as a direct consequence of their time in office; or scrupulous documentation of the dates, time, and content of conversations between ministers and businessmen such that even the most gradual accretion of influence might be detailed.

On the other hand, an end to contact between business and government would be nonsensical. Business provides the state's bread and butter. Government needs to develop a sound understanding of what business needs; and both sides will benefit from an exchange of administrative techniques, outlooks and experience. Nor does insulation mean insisting on strict propriety within business and government. Indeed, some writers argue that corruption in specific areas of government may be tackled by altering specific (and fairly technical) aspects of the political economy such that practices run with the prevailing current. In response to the problem of collusion between taxpayers and tax officials to understate their tax liabilities, Toye and Moore (1998) argue that

> 'earned income is positively and causally associated with states that are (a) effective, in the sense of exercising sovereignty, and (b) responsive to citizens, partly to the extent of being more democratic. We argue here that the same conceptual framework can help us understand how states treat their taxation systems and bureaucracies, and, therefore, the ways in which they may respond to pressures or opportunities to reform those systems to reduce corruption' (p.66). [*]

---

[*] See also: Moore, M. (1998).

By earned income they mean revenue – such as business turnover taxes and income taxes - that government has had to work for. This contrasts with low earned or unearned incomes such as taxes on, say, rights to extract oil and other natural resources or profits from overvalued exchange rates. The extent to which income is 'earned' finds expression both in the degree of organisational effort (in the size, efficiency, and differentiation of the bureaucratic apparatus), and in the extent of reciprocity (the benefits which citizens secure from their tax contributions).

Earned income is not incompatible with the presence of corrupt officials and taxpayers. Dishonesty there may be, but that dishonesty is predictable, controllable and organised, precisely because the collection of earned income requires a high degree of competency and efficiency. Moreover, the government's dependence on its citizens for its income, provides citizens with considerable leverage to compel government to spend their money according to their wishes. It is in these circumstances that anticorruption reform is most likely to be instigated and most likely to succeed. Again, this contrasts with a state in which government income is 'unearned'. Here, most revenues tend to be gathered from a few areas of economic activity (such as oil extraction), and government has little interest in other areas. Indeed, the revenue service may be treated as a pasture on which government supporters (or troublesome opponents) may be left to graze. In short, the harder a government has to work to collect its taxes, the greater the incentive to implement anticorruption reform and to do so successfully.

One implication of this argument, presumably, is that the diversification of the economy and greater interest in 'earned' categories of taxation should be encouraged. When a government's revenues are already earned, then the best measure, according to Toye and Moore, is to simplify the tax system. Corrupt officials prefer multiple and overlapping tax jurisdictions, complex eligibility criteria, discretionary procedures, and the full investigation of cases. Tax reform should therefore move in the opposite direction. It should aim to reduce: overlapping jurisdictions; the complexity of the tax structure (through, for example, the introduction of VAT of the tax credit type); and the frequency of face-to-face contacts between collector and payer. It then becomes possible to remove some of the uncertainty surrounding the true liability of the tax payer and, consequently, to weaken the incentive to offer bribes in return for discretionary rulings in favour of the tax payer. These measures have a good chance of working effectively, though it is unlikely that they will eradicate corruption entirely. And there are drawbacks: they do not necessarily lower the financial costs of collection; and there is likely to be resistance from officials.

When revenues are unearned, however, then the value of these kinds of solutions is questionable. In these circumstances, Toye and Moore point us to Flatters' and Macleod's (1995) argument that a degree of tolerance may be necessary. It is suggested that tax collectors (who have a better knowledge of true liabilities on the street) should be allowed to take bribes to supplement their wages. The *quid pro quo* for such latitude is that they deliver higher revenues to the central ministry. Those revenues will not be as large as they could be in a perfect world; but they will be better that any returned by entirely honest collectors on low salaries and with little incentive to inform the centre of the true liabilities of taxpayers.

2.1 Criticisms

If we set aside the more radical solutions advocated in (i), then it is difficult to quibble with the intentions and general direction of the solutions outlined in (ii). They ask us to set out more clearly what is, and what is not, acceptable; to insulate officials from temptations; to protect them from mischievous allegations; to improve the chances they will be discovered should they become corrupt; to raise the status of officials; to deepen their pride in themselves and in their institutions; and, where necessary, to follow the grain of more positive trends already present within the political economy.

However, there are a number of general problems with these kinds of structural solutions. One is the demand which they make on funds, on training, on political and bureaucratic processes (such as the need to secure budgetary appropriation and slots in the legislative calendar), on the energy of officials, and on the patience of both officials and those whom they govern. Indeed, so much time and effort may be required, that the encouragement of propriety seems to become an end in itself, while other matters are left unattended. A degree of imperfection and rule-bending is inevitable, perhaps necessary, in a poor country where government must act quickly and direct finite amounts of time, energy and money on keeping more and more people alive for a little longer.

A second general problem with structural adjustments is the assumption that there exists already a high degree of probity and institutional loyalty, and that most citizens themselves possess and respect those qualities. Even if technically correct and perfectly drafted, further legislation, the creation and elaboration of systems of oversight, and the clarification of rules, roles, responsibilities and functions, only mean something if those whom they concern are prepared to abide by them. But what if those circumstances do not prevail, and if institutional weakness is endemic? Where the upper echelons are corrupt, and where the lower ranks of officialdom and citizenry regard corruption as a customary fee for government workers on low salaries, then reform will prove extraordinarily difficult. We might assume that new rules, procedures and agencies, will remain uncorrupted; but unless these assumptions can be sustained, then all that may be achieved is a constant layering of ineffective agencies and processes and, through their accretion, the formation of an increasingly heavy and labyrinthine bureaucracy. Anticorruption measures will either be ignored or, most probably, used by political and bureaucratic factions to undermine or remove their opponents.

Before long, no one will remember where the truth was laid. The frustrations which mount in the wake of this fruitless expense of time and patience may only lead us back towards more radical or reactionary solutions: either the overthrow of the whole edifice, or the legalisation and justification of the interests of whoever happens to be powerful and wealthy. These solutions are no more likely to result in any improvement. Neither the retraction nor expansion of state powers, nor the managed or free market, offer a panacea. Corruption was a problem in socialist systems even before they began their attempts at capitalist transition; and it is no stranger either to military rule or to democracy.

3.0 Cultural measures

Johnston (1998) makes a very similar point:

> 'Where corruption is the exception, not the rule, reformers have several advantages. Anti-corruption laws, agencies and organisations are in place and enjoy broad-based support, as do independent courts, auditors and news media. Citizens and organisations are willing to confront the problem directly and elected officials cannot ignore them without the risk of losing office... Government is broadly legitimate; civil liberties, systems of accountability, property and contract rights, and the rule of law are credible' (p.85-86).

But where corruption is 'embedded in political and economic systems in ways that both reflect its impact and help sustain its force', it is transformed into a qualitatively different phenomenon. In these circumstances 'new institutional forms and procedures – like the ones they replace, in many instances - are often deprived of the administrative and political support and underlying normative consensus that they require for success' (*ibid.* p.86).

In other words, institutional reforms, revised technical and bureaucratic procedures, and additional layers of oversight, have a good chance of success when institutional loyalties are strong, and in these circumstances they may be valuable. But where the base of values, beliefs and loyalty which would otherwise sustain and defend propriety is weak or absent, then reform of institutions is unlikely to help. In this event, the kinds of structural measures we have already mentioned will have to follow or, at the very least, accompany efforts to stimulate a change in culture.

It is not easy, however, to pin down what we mean by culture or cultural measures; nor is the point at which culture ends and an institution begins either clear or certain. The problem we face is not merely one of semantics: how can we encourage the context needed to ensure the success of institutional reforms unless a distinction between structure and culture is apparent and unless we have an understanding of the direction and nature of the influence that each has upon the other? It might be argued that cultural measures must come first; yet, equally, structural reforms may be necessary to bring about cultural change.

We could, therefore, argue over whether the kinds of measures outlined below are indeed cultural or institutional. On the other hand, can we rule out the possibility that these concerns may only be a distraction? Perhaps what matters in the end is whether or not such measures prompt those who hold office in the public or private sectors to behave under their own volition in ways that squeeze corruption out of the system. Is this, perhaps, the acid test for any change that we might like to call 'cultural'?

3.1 Encouraging civil society

Johnston (1998) uses the term social empowerment to describe the strengthening of groups and interests that make up civil society (the organisations, enterprises and informal social networks which inhabit the gap between the individual and government) such that the range of political and economic resources open to ordinary citizens are expanded and protected (p.87). The strengthening of civil society works to reduce corruption primarily, but not only, through the conflicts which it generates between itself and government. These conflicts may grow out of private self-interest; but the settlements which emerge between public and private parties are more legitimate and desirable precisely because those interests have been engaged. In this process, civil society may serve as a communication link between government and people (*ibid.* p.91-92).

But how do we strengthen social empowerment? The strategies for doing so are, to some extent, determined by the nature of civil society.

(i) First, it is clear that state and civil society should achieve a balance of power, and that their subsequent development should retain that balance. If civil society is weak and the state is strong, then civil society will be left open to exploitation by political and bureaucratic monopolies. If the state is weak and civil society is strong, then government power and public officials will be exploited by the private interests of civil society: political institutions will be diverted in support of certain private interests. Civil society, then, must be developed in tandem with the state. Given this requirement, and given the fact that the development of civil society will be disorderly (this must be so if conflict and competition are to thrive), then effective political leadership together with effective legal and political sanctions (to be used against the corrupt) are also required.

(ii) Second, the balanced development of civil society and state will require extensive interactions between private parties and government. This will need to be arranged in such a way as to encourage mutual respect: citizens must know and value the duties and functions of officials; officials should respect the rights of citizens; and both should come to regard 'legitimate procedures as serving mutual ends' (*ibid.* p.94). Citizens' commitments to established rules should be encouraged by monitoring competition between private interests and by giving citizens a stake in the fruits and processes of government. For instance, more effective and open taxation makes it possible to see just how government works, how much it costs to run, and how working together in order to make the system more efficient is in everyone's interest. In these ways interactions between civil society and state are also likely to be made more predictable and orderly, salaries for officials will be easier to agree on, and the introduction of officially-recognised fees for government services made less contentious.

(iii) Strengthening social empowerment also requires that a balance is struck between political and economic opportunities. Following Huntingdon (1968), Johnston argues that where economic opportunities are plentiful and political opportunities scarce, people will try to buy their way into political power. Conversely, where political opportunities are abundant and economic opportunities are few and far between, people will use political power to enrich themselves. A balance between the economy and polity is therefore essential. Where corruption is endemic, however, the political economy is, almost by definition, unbalanced; there is also little competition (civil society is either weak or has concentrated power into its own hands); and the boundaries between state and civil society are blurred. How, then, do we gain a foothold and begin reform? Part of the answer is to introduce civil liberties. This will stimulate greater interaction between civil society and government, and will enable those who have lost out as a result of corruption to pursue remedies openly and directly. Another part of the answer is to attach credible guarantees to property and contract rights; and to funnel aid into emergent sectors of the economy.

(iv) Once civil liberties are secure it will also be possible to mobilize opinion against corruption. Specific institutions and methods are not always easily transplanted from one culture to the next: but public awareness campaigns which set out clear ethical standards, explain why transgression is damaging, and encourage civic participation (such as reporting incidents of possible corruption), are thought to be an important weapon against corruption. A still more fundamental way of mobilising opinion is to reach citizens early in their lives at school or at university. The aim here, again, is to establish a clear consensus on the meaning of corruption and to make people sensitive to the damage that it can do to them personally and to society more generally.

3.2 Criticisms

Although it may be possible to alter what are held to be the cultural features underlying corruption, there are a number of problems associated with this emphasis. The demand for political leadership and for legal and political sanctions; the requirement that civil society and the government respect each other and regard legitimate procedures as a means to a common ends; the introduction of more effective taxation; the introduction and observance of official fees; the introduction and protection of civil liberties, property and contract rights; and effective public awareness campaigns: all must surely presuppose fairly high levels of probity and institutional loyalty and the presence of the very patterns of behavior and values which these measures are supposed to stimulate and inculcate. The point is emphasised by Johnston's argument that these various measures should be complemented by all kinds of institutional and procedural developments, including the strengthening of investigative and prosecutorial powers; controls on campaign spending and on monopolies (economic and political); and the expansion of the electorate and the secret ballot. The argument that necessary cultural change will emerge from conflict between civil society and state as the two sides hammer out agreed values and agreed ways of organising politics and government, also requires much more elaboration and detail. After all, is it not possible that competition and conflict will lead to a further intensification of corruption as individuals and groups work to defend and expand their interests? Indeed, it might be said that the whole argument is only another form of words to describe governments (probably democratic) that are learning to respond to the demands and wishes of their constituents. The solution which we are being presented with is, in effect, democracy. But is democracy a solution or does an effective democracy presuppose a fairly clean state?

3.3 Sustainable controls

Galtung's (1998) remedies might take us more in the right direction. He notes that while most countries provide laws and sanctions against corruption, those laws are flouted and sanctions are infrequently imposed where corruption is endemic; and that the response aims to increase transparency and strengthen accountability in the public sector through public programmes, civil service reform, law enforcement, and anticorruption institutions. Galtung, in common with Johnston, also notes that institutional reform, while an important step, is not sufficient: its effects are usually fairly localised and do not usually last beyond the lives of the reformers. Sustainable controls on corruption are needed – strategies that will reduce endemic corruption to levels which are sporadic and tolerable and will keep things that way. The strategies he envisages comprise three parts.

The first is to identify and encourage stakeholders. Galtung begins with Klitgaard (1991) who questions the notion that corruption involves only two parties: the one who offers a bribe and the one who takes it. Klitgaard argues that, in fact, corruption involves three actors: the principal (or state); the agent (who works for the principal); and client (or citizen). Galtung suggests that this categorisation can be refined further. The principal may include both state and citizens (or clients); and agents may be understood to comprise politicians and civil servants. All may be corrupt and all must be engaged (through, say, Transparency International's Integrity Pact) in ways to put a stop to it. Reform, then, may originate from principals, agents, and clients.

The second part of Galtung's strategy is to establish credibility and feasibility. Reform, in other words, has to be both credible and feasible. The former criterion presupposes sound incentives and moral integrity, while the latter criterion presupposes legal, economic, political and civil viability. In navigating the difficult gradient between the two, reformers will have implement measures which balance an institution's credibility with its operational capacity. Galtung uses the example of Hong Kong's ICAC: through a law which granted a general amnesty, but which, for major instances of graft, made exceptions (such as the extradition of a former police commissioner from the UK), the ICAC was able to demonstrate its operational feasibility without losing its credibility.

The third part is the development and integration of international corruption controls. Corruption is not, and has never been, confined to a particular part of the world or to countries at one or other stage of development. In view of this, and given also the mobile and international nature of business and trade, it is easy to understand why an international dimension is needed. Bribes may be offered by international business organisations, and corrupt officials can fly overseas or move their takings quickly between accounts in many different countries. Tackling these kinds of cross-border exchanges and movements is likely to embroil national governments is all kinds of sensitive matters including extradition, the repatriation of the proceeds of corruption, cross-border legal assistance and investigations, and the harmonisation of sanctions and definitions. If domestic efforts to combat corruption are going to be fully effective and if international links to prevent cross-border corruption are to be strengthened, then countries will have to coordinate their actions and strategies. We might add that international measures exert an important external discipline on national governments to deal with their own problems of corruption in a way and to an extent that otherwise they might not have done. And indeed, measures to curb bribery and corruption are now on national and international agendas. These measures include: the OECD (Organisation for Economic Cooperation and Development)'s Convention on Combating the Bribery of Foreign Public Officials in International Business Transactions; the Council of Europe's Criminal Law Convention of 1998, its Civil Law Convention on Corruption of 1999, and its Treaty on the Protection of Financial Interests of the Community of 1995; and the UN's 1988 Convention Against Illicit Traffic in Narcotic Drugs.

Galtung's strategy does not get away from a need to presuppose degrees of integrity and organisational strength. But it explicitly recognises this problem, and it seems to offer a realistic foothold: those involved in corruption may be assumed to come from all levels of institutions (political, economic and civil); and it is they who are often best placed to deal with it. Anticorruption policies need to incorporate fine judgment and a degree of tolerance.

4.0 A holistic approach?

If we are to deal with corruption then it would seem that we require a holistic approach which draws in the state, the private sector, and civil society. Various combinations of measures are suggested in the literature, [*] aimed mainly at reducing the opportunities and incentives for corruption, and at changing the culture within organisations and in society more generally. The courses of action more commonly suggested are listed below.

(i) Reducing and simplifying bureaucratic functions and procedures; making transparent the rules and procedures governing investments (especially by foreign businesses) and bids for public contracts; clarifying and simplifying accounting and auditing rules; and drawing up and promulgating codes of ethics.

(ii) Improving the pay, conditions and status of officials; paring down the discretion of officials; a layering of cross-checking and monitoring procedures; the rotation of officials; strengthening dedicated internal oversight units (especially those responsible for monitoring spending); and establishing or reinforcing external and independent oversight bodies.

(iii) Establishing investigative agencies; weeding out mischievous allegations; the professional investigation of allegations with possible substance, followed (if

---

[*] See, in particular, Klitgaard, 1991; and Bhargava and Bolongaita, 2004

there is indeed a case to answer) by vigorous prosecutions regardless of the rank and standing of the accused; and levying penalties commensurate with the offence.

(iv) Ensuring the impartiality of the judiciary; introducing witness protection programmes; and strengthening law enforcement agencies.

(v) Encouraging cultural change through, say, schools and universities where values conducive to effective institutional life may be instilled and communicated; launching public education campaigns, both to heighten awareness of the damage wrought by corruption and to encourage people to report possible offences; identifying and supporting those officials who are 'clean'; and converting networks of corruption into more positive and constructive patterns of behavior.

(vi) Encouraging the media, NGOs, and the public, to monitor, scrutinize and report on the actions, behaviour and decisions of government and private businesses; the careful recording of meetings, especially those concerned with the formulation and implementation of policy and legislation, or in which businesses or other interest groups participate; and introducing freedom of information laws.

(vii) Coordinating the activities of the public sector, private sector, and civil society with international organisations in order to develop synergies in programme design and implementation at local, national, and international levels.

In short, efforts to remove incentives for corruption, to strengthen oversight, and to balance out competing interests, must take place alongside the liberation and development of civil society and should be given an international dimension.

4.1 Problems?

Although these solutions may appear satisfying - especially when set within a rounded institutional, cultural and international context - they have not managed to shake themselves free of our earlier doubts. In particular, this holistic approach still sounds very much like the description of a state in which institutional loyalties and an adherence to laws, rules, procedure and conventions are already strong. Put another way, its solutions - both structural and cultural - assume that probity is widespread and that there is common agreement on the focus and purpose of organisations. Certainly it may be argued that if institutions are firm enough, and are defined sharply enough, for corruption to have become a noticeable problem, then a degree of institutional loyalty must be present. It is therefore probable that institutional reform will have some effect, and that cultural change may be propagated through existing structures. Yet this may be to assume too much, in which case a determination to impose and harden institutional formality is only likely to make matters worse. This is so in a number of ways. One is the use of these 'reforming' bodies, laws, and procedures both to undermine political enemies and to shroud one's own improprieties. A common response to the politicisation of institutions and processes which were designed originally to eradicate and mitigate corruption, is to roll out another layer of oversight bodies, investigative agencies, and monitoring procedures. When this layer is politicised too, yet another is unfurled. As this layering of agencies and procedures thickens, it soon becomes impossible to know where the truth lies; and trust between politicians and citizens is ended.

5.0 An attitudinal perspective

We have noted that solutions to corruption tend to assume that a degree of probity and institutional loyalty are already in place. Yet where corruption is endemic, this is precisely the assumption that we cannot make. How, then, is it possible to formulate and implement measures on a bed of corrupt behaviour which renders those measures ineffective?

Earlier in this book we argued that attitudinal change underlies the professionalisation of organisations. This change may be spontaneous; but it may also be encouraged by the practical demands made upon us as we attempt to put together and sustain organisations and procedures with certain qualities. These demands may lead us into a virtuous circle of shifting attitudes, changes in representations, and increasingly professional organisations.

More specifically, we have argued (see, also, Hodder 2006) that a strongly personalistic (or instrumental) attitude towards relationships - associated with limited representations of a malleable world focussed on self - produces unstable, poorly focussed, and (in reaction, as authoritarianism is imposed) arthritic bodies. Personalism and authoritarianism also generate a strong sense of alienation within and outside those institutions.

It is partly in response to this alienation that social relationships among the institutions' members are, outside the institution, treated increasingly *as if* important in their own right. Associated with this shift in members' attitudes are representations of a less malleable world focussed outside self. And it is in partly in defense of this deepening social refuge that, within the institution or organisation, relationships are transformed conceptually into rules and roles which are treated explicitly as phenomena quite independent of relationships practiced outside the institution. Yet the true social quality of rules and roles (which make up the walls and frame of the institution) is recognized *implicitly*: for were this social quality to be made explicit, then the instrumental treatment of relationships would have been openly admitted; and were this social quality to be denied entirely, then the institution's rules and roles would have been transformed into pure absolutes – instruments valuable to those in authority, but which would begin to return the institution toward a more personalistic and authoritarian condition. In this way the social sphere (outside the institution) is protected.

Meanwhile, within the institution, precision, congruency and stability can be brought to the members' developing representations of their place within the institution, of the institution and its rules and roles, and of the institution's place in the wider world. These qualities are essential if behaviour within the institution is to be coordinated, dovetailed, and focussed.

This experience - the distancing of relationships and the treatment of institutions *as if* absolute - is taken by members into their wider social lives (family and friends), civic associations (charity, community, educational and 'non-governmental'), and into other bureaucratic, political or economic institutions (as, say, the bureaucrat helps out in the family business, or as the businessman is brought into bureaucratic or political institutions). This works both to deepen still further the social sphere (and, therefore, a concern for others and community); and to spread increasingly professional behaviour throughout civic, economic, political, bureaucratic, and judicial institutions.

Attitudinal change, then, is some extent endogenous: it is generated within each of us and within our institutions. Moreover - and this is a vital point - institutions which stimulate attitudinal change appear do so incidentally. That is, attitudinal change is side-effect arising from their everyday workings. We might expect, therefore, that there are always hotspots of change: clusters of individuals appearing within institutions (even the more corrupt or authoritarian of them) whose attitudes are already conducive to the professionalisation of those institutions.

A three-part strategy immediately suggests itself. The first to link these clusters together. Drawn together in mutual support and recognition they become part of the spread and enlargement of hotspots working to shift attitudes within the population towards a critical mass - at which moment the distancing of relationships, probity, and professionalism, become normal and expected. Left unconnected, unrecognized, and bombarded by cynical representations of the political economy, the people who comprise these clusters will feel dejected and wonder why they should remain either competent or honest. The second part of the strategy requires us: to support those organisations whose workings happen to stimulate attitudinal change; to encourage the proliferation of similar organisations; to identify those practices and representations which stimulate change within those organizations; and to propagate these practices and representations more widely. The third part is to highlight the good which already exists within the political economy; and in this and in other ways to construct and disseminate more positive representations through the media, schools, universities, and civil associations.

This three-part strategy does not exclude more usual methods with their focus on detection, prosecution, the removal of incentives, and supervision: but it does have certain advantages. Since the organisations which encourage attitudinal change do so almost incidentally (as a by-product of their everyday operations and their pursuit of quite unrelated objectives), and since this change occurs even within authoritarian and corrupt institutions, then there is no need for a wholesale redirection of government policy and effort. Indeed, the kinds of organisations and practices which we have suggested may stimulate change are very likely to be part of current development efforts (such as the promotion of small family businesses).

Furthermore, this three-part strategy tackles corruption indirectly. It focuses on the identification and promotion of certain kinds of practices, attitudes representations which often appear to have little to do with anticorruption drives. Frequent and direct confrontation and scrutiny may help only to breed negative representations whose influence will be counterproductive. Suspicion and distrust is likely to foster alienation, resentment, and resistance; and every mistake, inefficiency and imperfection will be read as a symptom of corruption. The ambitious will have been handed a means to undermine their opponents, while the honest will have little choice but to suffer in silence.

5.1 Method

Whilst our perspective offers a possible strategy, it also presents us with a number of immediate demands. We must demonstrate that representations, attitudes and practices work as we say they do, or, more accurately, that the play we have set out provides an effective interpretative framework; that hotspots of change are present and will, if encouraged, have the influence that we say they will have; and that members of organisations do indeed carry their experiences with them as they move among institutions, communities, and kin and friendship groups, and there influence, and are influenced by, other people.

We can formulate these demands into two objectives. The first is to demonstrate that the workings of institutions - and their role in wider social change - may be understood with reference to the play of representations, attitudes (to social relationships) and practice. The second is to demonstrate: that the day-to-day operations of political, bureaucratic, and economic institutions happen to produce social changes (alterations in attitudes, representation and practice) among their members which contribute to those institutions' professionalisation; [*] and that, through their members' lives outside institutions, these changes permeate wider society where still other stimuli will, through that same route, find their way back into institutions. So how do we begin to meet these demands?

The suggested method is divided into five parts, and refers to the case of the Philippines. (I) The *first* is to set out common official, journalistic and scholarly representations of the Philippines' political economy. These representations are

---

[*] 'Professionalisation' we have defined as the 'distancing' of social relationships through the performance of our masquerade, and, consequently, as the defense of the integrity of the institution and the social sphere.

likely to influence, as well as draw from, the representations held by the analysts and by the people in whom the analysts are interested. This entails constructing from documentary materials (official, academic and journalistic):

(i) an official, technical account of working and significance of specific institutions (economic, political, bureaucratic and civic), detailing their organisation, functions, codes of conduct, conventions, oversight and other monitorial mechanisms, and other core procedures and processes; (ii) a broader academic account of the historical development and current organisation and workings of institutions; (iii) profiles (educational, political, professional and commercial) of key personnel and their families; (iv) details of interconnections – kinship, shared business interests (including land ownership), and shared experience and loyalties (such as attendance at the same schools, universities, military classes, civic associations) – across and within businesses, civic associations, and the main branches of government; and (v) the legislative history of politicians, cross-referenced with family and business interests.

(II) This material would also inform the initial selection of organizations, communities and individuals for surveys and interviews. Legislative, executive, bureaucratic and judicial organizations would be selected according to their political significance and their role in the key financial, spending, decision-making, and oversight functions of the state as detailed in official, acadmic and journalistic representations. The organisations initially selected would, ideally, include: the Legislature; the Office of the President; the Departments of Finance, Budget and Management, Health, Education, Public Works and Highways, and Interior and Local Government; the Central Bank; the Civil Service Commission; the Commission on Elections; the Commission on Audit; the Ombudsman; the Committee on Appointments; the Judicial and Bar Council; and the Supreme Court. Businesses would be selected according to their economic importance as indicated by sales and assets (such that small local businesses, as well those that rank among the nation's top 100 firms, are included); their form of ownership (corporate, family, single, partnership); ethnicity and nationality; and their documented links with government, bureaucracy, and civic associations. The selection of associations (or civil organizations) would be determined by their connexions with state and business organizations.

The selection of personnel within these organizations would aim (in line with official representations of these organisations' composition) to achieve a balance in status, role, and rank (higher, middle, and lower), and in the extent of individuals' connexions with other institutions (from extensive to minimal or absent).

In addition to these organizations (state, business and civil), we would also want to select a small number of local *communities* (*barangay*-level and *purok*-level). Here selection would be determined by a preponderance of members without, or with only limited, experience of working within state, business and civil organizations. This may help to indicate (and we put it no more strongly) the possible significance of the particular attitudes, representations and practices exhibited by those who comprise state, business or civil organizations. The selection of a further two communities would be determined in part by a preponderance of connexions with state, business and civil organizations.

Rolling contacts and multiple triangulations would determine the initial selection of the family and friends of members of organizations. And while the need to keep a balance between institutions, families, and friendship circles, age, sex, rank and the position of subjects will be kept in mind, rolling contacts and traiangulation will also determine the subsequent selection of state, business and civil organizations and their individual members.

(III) The third part comprises attempts to elicit (a) attitudes and (b) representations. The aim of (a) is to provide a basic sketch of the mental states (the attitudes and coarse representations) which inform, and are informed by, the practices of the members of selected institutions. The aim of (b) is to provide more detail on these representations and attitudes, and to examine their play with practice.

(a) There exists within the literature an extensive array of established attitudinal scales. The meaning of the scores which these tests for attitude yield must be treated with care. In chapter 4 we drew attention to a number of questions often associated with attitudinal scales. For instance, is there a direct connection between stated attitudes and subsequent action? And are there no cultural differences in the meaning of attitudes? We also noted that we reserve the term 'attitudes' to describe our social relationships; that qualities or states of mind often described as attitudes are better understood as representations; and that whilst attitudes give an indication of our representations of past action and (to the extent that they may inform our subsequent behavior) may provide us with an indication of future action, neither our attitudes nor representations enable us to predict subsequent behavior. Nevertheless, these tests have been used widely, and they may prove themselves to be quite valuable in the field. If so, then further discussion on the merits and demerits associated with these tests will be needed.

Certain tests purport to assess directly attitudes to the manipulation of other people (commonly referred to as Machiavellianism scales), and attitudes to self and others more generally. There are also tests to asses: attitudes to family along an autocratic-democratic continuum; degrees of alienation; and attitudes to institutions (or what, through our attitudinal perspective, we would describe as our representations of institutions). These might help us to assess attitudes (to relationships) indirectly, for we have argued that feelings of alienation, authoritarianism, cynicism, and distrust, are likely to accompany shifts in attitude towards the personal. And because these scales commonly present respondents with lists of varying statements about self, others and world from which to choose,[*] they might also help us to elicit somewhat rough (but perhaps telling) representations from large numbers of people. A sketch of the attitudes and coarse representations prevalent among an institution's membership would also help us to select individuals for more detailed analyses of the kinds outlined in (b).

(b) There also exists an extensive literature on methods used to elicit detailed representations. These include, for example, multi-dimensional scaling, scenarios, and semantic differentials. However, it is the more ethnographic techniques which seem best suited to our attitudinal perspective. Two methods in particular suggest themselves to this study. The first comprises free descriptions or, in other words, the accounts (written and diagrammatic) provided by individuals of the organization and their place within it, of the organisation's place in a wider institutional pattern, and of the problems faced by the organization and its staff (together with possible solutions). The second comprises free and open-ended interviews during which similar questions are pursued in more detail. Contradictory representations - drawn either from other earlier interviews or from our composite documentary representations - might also be introduced into the discussion to stimulate, test, and compare the interviewee's representations.

The precise details of the surveys and interviews are subject to change following trial runs. But we would envisage that the surveys would comprise batteries of attitudinal scales which attempt to measure, in particular, attitudes to self and others, instrumentalism, alienation, family, and authoritarianism. Interviews would focus on individuals from three groups (see part **II** above): *[a]* members of political, economic and civic organization; *[b]* families and friends of members of

---

[*] For instance, Kelley's (1934) scale, which was designed to measure attitudes to institutions, provides some 90 statements ranging from, say, 'encourage social improvement' to 'developing into a racket'.

group *[a]*; and *[c]* members of local communities. These interviews will, in general, attempt to elicit from members of institutions and their family and friends, and from communities, their own accounts of: their own and other members' *attitudes (to relationships)*; their *representations* of the particular organisation, family, friendship circle and communities in which they work and live, of their place within it, and of the wider institutional pattern of the political economy; the *practices* which constitute their place and role within institution, family and friendship circles, and community. As they do so, interviews within each group (*[a]*, *[b]* and *[c]*) will concentrate on the following matters:

[a]. An interviewee's own account of:

(i) the organisation and its functions; its workings (procedures conventions, rules, constraints, oversight, and short-cuts); its connections with other institutions and place in the wider institutional pattern; problems, improvements and changes;

(ii) the member's own role, way of working, and place within the institution and wider institutional pattern; the role and working of others; self and others; relationships with, and behaviour towards, colleagues within the institution and in other institutions; tensions, constraints, and oversight; promotions and ambitions;

(iii) the significance of kinship; inheritance of posts; significance of ethnicity, language, and place of origin;

(iv) their own and other members' business, political, bureaucratic and civic interests and experience;

[b]. An interviewee's account of:

(i) their place and role within in their family and friendship groups; qualities of, relationships with, and responsibilities to, friends and family members; tensions, rivalry and ambitions; (ii) what interviewee from group *[a]* has brought to, and learnt from, group *[b]*; the extent to which *[a]*'s experiences are carried from institutions to *[b]*, and *vice versa*.

[c]. Interviewee's account of: (i) networks of kinship and friendship; (ii) the organisation, functions and working of *barangays* and *puroks*, their interconnections with other institutions, and their place in the wider pattern of political and economic institutions; (iii) roles, status and hierarchy within these networks of relationships and broader institutional patterns; (iv) the significance of ethnicity, language, kinship, and place of origin.

(IV) Part four would consider the statistical significance of the data generated by the surveys and by the content analysis of interviews. For instance, are measures for instrumentalism correlated with measures for, say, anomie, authoritarianism, or representations of particular institutions? We should emphasise that it would not be our intention here to present statistical significance as evidence in support of an interpretation reached through our attitudinal perspective. We have in chapter 2 already referred to doubts over the use of statistical analyses in this way. Our intention is: to look for non-conforming data; and to consider alternative interpretations of data even when such data provide a good fit with those interpretations offered by our attitudinal perspective. In short, statistical treatment of data is used to prompt interpretations other than, and perhaps conflicting with, our attitudinal perspective. If statistical data should appear to provide a good fit with our perspective, or if it should point only weakly to other possibilities, then this would be viewed neutrally rather than considered as supporting evidence for our interpretation. That is, our 'take' of any apparent validation which statistical treatments may yield is viewed not as proof, but as the absence of a reason to put to one side, or to alter, our interpretative framework.

It is in this sprit that we would also draw in a range of contrasting and often conflicting theoretical and conceptual debates and interpretations. This critical and dimensional approach is less likely to determine the interpretation of evidence; it is also more likely to leave open the selection of observations which do not 'fit' initial expectations, and to generate unplanned, unexpected and potentially valuable ideas and interpretations. In addition to extensive materials on corruption (examples of which we have already touched on in this book), four intersecting bodies of literature (elements of which of have also been discussed in this pages) would, at this stage of the research, seem to be of particular relevance.

(i) The Philippines' political economy from patron-client frameworks to patrimonialism and beyond, together with more generic analyses of political and economic transformation.

(ii) Notions of intentionality, reference and representation, from Brentano and Dilthey, to Frege and Fodor, to the work of social psychologists such as Moscovici, Jodelet, Abric, and Doise.

(iii) Institutional change, organizational theory, and the Human Relations school of management with its notion of neo-human relationships.

(iv) Anthropological and sociological perspectives on social change: from Radcliffe-Brown, Firth, Fortes, Malinowski, the Wilsons, Leach and Herskovits, to more recent ethnographic approaches to transition, global processes, and public-private distinctions (such as Gupta and Herzfeld); and from Weber and Durkheim, to Giddens and the post-modern view that there can be no consensus of interpretation.

(V) In part five we begin to construct our accounts of the workings of political, bureaucratic and economic institutions, of how and why they are professionalised and made effective, and of their role in wider social change. Our surveys will provide us with a sketch of the attitudes and representations which characterise particular institutions and communities, while the techniques outlined in III (b) will give us a more detailed picture of those representations and attitudes and their play with practice.

However, it is important to reiterate that our written accounts of practice are also constructed from our subjects' representations of their own and other people's actions, from documentation (official, journalistic and academic), and from our own observations. Our accounts of practice (and its play with attitudes and representations) are serviceable, but they are no more than representations. They are influenced by our own attitudes, prior representations, and practices, just as interpretations of our written accounts are influenced by the mental states and practices of the interpreter. The extent to which our accounts are, or are not, bound into the thought of our readers and influence practice, may also have a bearing on their subsequent interpretation. We are compelled, therefore, to think about how we might assess: the influence which our own attitudes, prior representations, and practices have had upon our writing; the possible effects which our accounts might have if bound into practice; and the influence which these effects might have upon subsequent re-interpretations of our accounts. We might suggest, most obviously, that we apply to ourselves the same batteries of surveys, interviews and analysis that were applied to our subjects. We might also want to put together detailed reports of what we believe our final published essays will look like, and submit these to our subjects for their comments. As much as this may reveal about our subjects, it may also tell us a good deal about ourselves. In these ways it might be possible: to understand, in some small measure, the influence which our own representations, attitudes and practices, have had on our analyses; to appreciate the dialectic between our analyses and our subjects; to add further dimensions to the representations yielded by our subjects; and to refine our accounts a little more. Thus we move to final publications that are but the start of a new cycle of dis-aggregation and reformulation.

6.0 Conclusions

In this chapter we have set out some of the more common and established thoughts about how we deal with corruption; and we have noted that a central problem with these solutions is that they assume a fair degree of institutional strength. A still deeper problem is also present. Earlier in this book we suggested that corruption is but a name we give to our interpretation of acts with which we disapprove, and which are set within a dimensional organic context. What we are trying to solve is neither fixed nor specific. It is a representation of acts with many dimensions viewed from many different angles. If we treat this representation as a phenomenon in its own right, we will succeed only in projecting upon the world vaporous images which, just as quickly as they seem to bubble up from the normal and unnoticeable, melt back into that substance. Our strategies and policy formulations, and our heavy institutions and processes, are too slow and awkward to capture, analyse, and deal with these phantasms.

We have also attempted, through our attitudinal perspective, to sketch out a possible approach to deal with the countless and dimensional acts, their antecedents and their effects, which we call corruption. We have argued that there are to be found, within and across institutions, pockets of individuals (some of whom may, conceivably, also be engaged in corruption) whose attitudes and representations of the world may be conducive to the strengthening of institutions. These hotspots may, occasionally, emerge spontaneously; but they are also generated by the routine operation of routine institutions, including those which may otherwise appear either weak or excessively authoritarian. Our task is to identify and explain these hotspots; and to consider how we might propagate and link them together, such that the people who comprise them are now presented with channels for mutual encouragement and support. Since these hotspots are to be found in many diverse lines of activity, we might imagine that these linkages will emerge across many kinds of apparently unrelated sectors. This is a distinct advantage: it is not the explicit aims or function of these organizations that matters, but that through their everyday workings they happen to stimulate attitudinal change and the formation of more positive representations of self and world. The more widely these seeds can be scattered, the more creative and intense the resulting synergies are likely to be. Other advantages would seem to derive from the indirect nature of this approach: it is less confrontational and less likely to send those who are (or who would be) corrupt running for cover; it is tolerant of those who are corrupt or who are more likely to act corruptly, and seeks to turn them rather than to punish them; it aims to enhance positive tendencies already at work within institutions; and, as a consequence, it is unlikely to demand the re-direction of a government's energy, time or money from its core duties and priorities on any scale. For all these reasons, it is less likely that these indirect measures will themselves become politicised. In short, this attitudinal approach may offer effective solutions at minimal political and economic cost.

None of this is to suggest that we put to one side more direct attacks on corruption: there will be those who cannot be persuaded to alter their behaviour except through fear of discovery and punishment; and, for the rest, temptation and shifts towards the personal are always present. The removal of incentives and the imposition of disincentives are all part of the solution, and part of the means through which effective organizations can be maintained. Yet emphasis should, for the reasons we have set out, lie with the identification and encouragement of hotspots, and with the creation of an atmosphere that is tolerant and creative.

The problem now is to demonstrate in the field that these hotspots exist and that they encourage change in the ways that we say they do. We have sketched out how this might be done. But, as always, the proof of the pudding is in the eating.

CHAPTER 6
Conclusions:
a meaning for corruption

In chapter 1 we argued that we might be better placed to define corruption only after we had considered its causes, effects and solutions in a little more detail. Over the last five chapters we have introduced a range of different perspectives and arguments on these matters. And we have, in particular, raised the suggestion that when we speak of 'corruption' we are speaking only of an idea or set of ideas. Corruption is, like all thoughts about ourselves and the world, a representation of the world and our place within it. As such it informs our practice (our relationships with each other); its details are, like all our representations, influenced by the practice we observe around us and in which we participate; and it is coloured by our attitudes to social relationships. When we speak of 'corruption', then, we speak of a representation that is part of the play of representations, practice and attitudes which constitutes the substance of our world.

Through this perspective we have offered our own particular representation of corruption. We have suggested that corruption is an expression of our humanity. This is so various senses. It reflects a shift in attitude away from the affect and towards the personal; and it is our experience of the personal that allows us to know and appreciate the affect intimately. Without the choice to eschew the treatment of our relationships (and our institutions, procedures and virtues) as expedients and, instead, to treat them to *as if* absolute, we cannot experience for ourselves the true meaning and importance of our relationships. Indeed, without that choice we are led into a Puritanical state - a cold world in which we are separated from our humanity. Puritanism, we have argued, emerges where the affect dominates. It begins once we lose sight of the importance of the masquerade: relationships, rules, roles, institutions and virtues are transformed into autonomous phenomena; we feel compelled to adhere to these symbols; and we demand that other people feel the same. In this way we make ourselves slaves to virtue and propriety. Compassion is poisoned; intolerance reigns; and, under the repression of self, an unacknowledged desire for a return to personalism gathers force. Blinded by a thick and heavy righteousness, we no longer know of the misery we inflict on others, nor do we care.

This, then, is what we have come to mean by corruption: it is a shift to the personal. Yet, as such, it is also the route to an intimate appreciation of virtue and propriety, and it is a defense against Puritanism. A number of features attend this meaning of corruption. First, there can be no rule book, no compendium, no list of proper or improper behaviour; but what is proper and virtuous in any particular instance will be understood as such by any one with a sense of propriety and virtue. Secondly, whilst corruption (and so immorality and impropriety) may be understood as a movement away from the affect and towards the personal, this movement is not necessarily associated with corrupt, improper and immoral behaviour in all instances. Thirdly, just as there is no list of proper or moral acts, so there is no list of corruption's effects, nor can there be any list of solutions to corruption. However, we have argued that attitudinal change may be spontaneous; and that it is a by-product of the everyday working of everyday institutions including those that are weak or excessively authoritarian. If we can identify these hotspots and link them together, if we can encourage the practices responsible for stimulating attitudinal change and more positive representations within those hotspots, and if we can bring these practices and representations into other organisations, then society may reach critical mass fairly quickly and at comparatively little economic and political cost. In these discussions we have also set out how this might be done. It is to the analysis and assessment of this practical work in the field that we turn next.

BIBLIOGRAPHY

Abric, J.C. 1993. Central system, peripheral system: their functions and roles in the dynamics of social representations. *Papers of Social Representations* 2: 75-78

Asian Development Bank. 1998. *Anticorruption Policy*. Manila

Banfield, E.C. 1958. *The Moral Basis of a Backward Society*. New York

_____ 1970. The moral basis of a backward society. In *Political Corruption*, ed. A,J. Heidenheimer. New Jersey

_____ 1975. Corruption as a feature of governmental organisation. *Journal of Law and Economics* XVIII: 587-605

Bardhan, P. 1997. Corruption and development: a review of issues. *Journal of Economic Literature* XXXV: 1320-1346

Bayley, D.H. 1966. The effects of corruption in a developing nation. *Western Political Quarterly* XIX: 719-732

Bell, D. 1976. *Cultural Contradictions of Capitalism*. Cambridge

Bhargava V. and Bolongaita E. 2004. *Challenging Corruption in Asia: case studies and a framework for action*. Washington, D.C.

Bicchieri, C. and Duffy, J. 1997. Corruption cycles. *Political Studies* XLV: 477-495

Bourdieu, P. 1980 *The Logic of Practice*. Cambridge

_____ 1990 *In Other Words*. Cambridge

Brentano, F. 1976. *Psychology from an Empirical Standpoint*. Volume 1. Edited by O. Kraus, and translated by L. McAlister *et al*. London

Brooks, R.C. 1910. *Corruption in American Politics*. New York. (Reproduced as 'The nature of political corruption', and as 'Apologies for political corruption', in *Political Corruption*, ed. A,J. Heidenheimer. New Jersey).

Brown, D. E. 1991. *Human Universals*. Philadelphia

Business Week. 1993. The destructive costs of greasing palms. December 6th

Callaghy, T.M. 1989. Toward state capability and embedded liberalism in the Third World: lessons for adjustment. In J.M. Nelson ed. *Fragile Coalitions: the politics of economic adjustment*. New Jersey.

Campos J.E., Lien D., and Pradhan S. 1999. The impact of corruption on investment: predictability matters. *World Development* 27: 1059-1067

Cartier-Bresson, J. 1997. Corruption networks, transaction security and illegal social exchange. *Political Studies* XLV: 463-476

Chen, A. H. Y. 1999. Rational law, economic development, and the case of China. *Social and Legal Studies* 8: 97-120

Collingwood, R.G. 1946. *The Idea of History.* Oxford

Crouch, H. 1985. *Economic Change, Social Structure, and Political Systems in Southeast Asia: Philippine development compared with other ASEAN countries.* Singapore

———— 1979. Patrimonialism and military rule in Indonesia. *World Politics* 31: 571-87

de Sardan, Olivier J.P. 1999. A moral economy of corruption in Africa? *Journal of Modern African Studies* 37: 25-52

Deaux, K. and Philogène, G. 2001. *Representations of the Social.* Oxford

Derrida, J. 1976. *Of Grammatology.* Baltimore

———— 1978. *Writing and Difference.* London

Dia, M. 1996. *Africa's Management in the 1990s and Beyond: reconciling indigenous and transplanted institutions.* Washington D.C.

Dilthey, W. 1976. *Selected Writings.* Cambridge. Edited and translated by H. Rickman

Dobel, J.P. 1978. The corruption of a state. *American Political Science Review* 72: 958-73

Doise, W. , Clémence, A. and Lorenzi-Cioldi, F. 1993. *The Quantitative Analysis of Social Representations.* London

Durkheim, E. 1984. *The Division of Labour.* Houndsmills

Duveen, G. and Lloyd, B. 1993. An ethnographic approach to social representations. In G. M. Breakwell and D.V. Canter eds. *Empirical Approaches to Social Representations.* Oxford

Eckstein, H. 1966. *Division and Cohesion in Democracy: study of Norway.* Princeton

Elias, N. 1994. *The Civilizing Process.* Oxford. Translated by Edmund Jephcott. Originally published in 1939, by Haus zum falker, Basel

Evans, P. 1992. The state as problem and solution: predation, embedded autonomy, and structural change. In S. Haggard and R.R. Kaufman eds. *The Politics of Economic Adjustment.* Princeton

———— 1989. Predatory, developmental and other apparatuses: a comparative political economy perspective on the Third World state. *Sociological Forum* 4: 561-587

Firth, R. 1951 *The Elements of Social Organisation.* London

Fisman R. and Gatti R. 2002. Decentralisation and corruption: evidence across countries. *Journal of Public Economics* 83: 325-345

Flatters F. and Macleod M. 1995. Administrative corruption and taxation. *International Tax and Public Finance* 2: 397-417

Fodor, J. 1987. *Psychosemantics: the problem of meaning in the Philosophy of Mind.* Cambridge, Mass.

Foucault, M. 1980. *Power-Knowledge*. Brighton

Friedrich, C.J. 1963. *Man and His Government*. New York

Galtung, F. 1998. Criteria for sustainable corruption control. In M. Robinson ed. *Corruption and Development*. London

Geach, P. and Black, M. eds. 1960. *Philosophical Writings of Gottlob Frege*. Oxford

Geertz, C. 1965. The impact of the concept of culture on the concept of man. In J. R. Platt ed. *New Views of the Nature of Man*. Chicago

Giddens, A. 1984. *The Constitution of Society*. Cambridge

_____ 1992. *The Transformation of Intimacy*. Cambridge

Girling, J. 1997. *Corruption, Capitalism and Democracy*. London

Goffman, E. 1963. *Behaviour in Public Places*. Glencoe, Ill.

Goudie, A.W. and Stasavage, D. 1998. A framework for the analysis of corruption. *Crime, Law and Social Change* 29: 113-59

Gray, C. 1979. Civil service compensation in Indonesia. *Bulletin of Indonesian Economic Studies* 15: 85-113

Guelke, L. 1974. An idealist alternative in human geography. *Annals of the Association of American Geographers* 64: 193-202

Gupta, A. 1995. Blurred boundaries: the discourses of corruption, the culture of politics, and the imagined state. *American Ethnologist* 22: 375-402

Haller D. and Shore C. 2005. *Corruption: anthropological perspectives*. London

Harris, C. 1978. The historical mind and the practice of geography. In Ley, D. and Samuels, M. eds. *Humanistic Geography*. London

Harris, R. 2003. *Political Corruption: in and beyond the nation state*. London

Heidenheimer, A.J. 1970 a. The context of analysis. In A.J. Heidenheimer, ed. *Political Corruption*. New Jersey.

_____ ed. 1970. *Political Corruption*. New Jersey.

Herzfeld, M. 1992. *The Social Production of Indifference: exploring the symbolic roots of western bureaucracy*. Chicago

Heywood, P. 1997. Political corruption: problems and perspectives. *Political Studies* XLV: 417-35

Hodder, R. 2000. *In China's Image: Chinese self-perception in Western thought*. New York

_____ 2002. *Between Two Worlds: society, politics and business in the Philippines*. London

_____ 1996. *Merchant Princes of the East: cultural delusions, economic success, and the Overseas Chinese in Southeast Asia*. London

_____ 2006. *Overseas Chinese and Trade Between the Philippines and China*. New York

Huntington, S. 1968. *Political Order in Changing Societies*. New Haven

_____ 1970. Modernization and corruption. In *Political Corruption*, ed. A,J. Heidenheimer. New Jersey

Hutchcroft, P. 1991. Oligarchies and cronies in the Philippine state: The politics of patrimonial plunder. *World Politics* 43:216–43

_____ 2001. Centralisation and decentralisation in administration and politics: assessing territorial dimensions of authority and power. *Governance* 14: 23-53

_____ 1994. Booty Capitalism: business-government relations in the *Philippines.* In Business and government in industrializing Asia, ed. A. MacIntyre. Ithaca

_____ 1997. The politics of privilege: assessing the impacts of rents, corruption and clientelism on Third World development. *Political Studies* XLV: 639-58

_____. 1998. *Booty Capitalism: the politics of banking in the Philippines.* Ithaca

Hutchings, G. 2001. *Modern China.* London

Jodelet, D. 1991. *Madness and Social Representations.* London

Johnston, M. 1998. Fighting systemic corruption: social foundations for institutional reform. In M. Robinson, ed. *Corruption and Development,* London

Kelley, I.B. 1934. Construction and validation of a scale to measure attitude towards any institution. *Purdue University Study of Higher Education* 35:18-36

Kerkvliet, B. J. 1995. Toward a more comprehensive analysis of Philippine politics: Beyond the patron-client, factional framework. *Journal of Southeast Asian Studies* 26:401–19

Khan, M.H. 1996. The efficiency implications of corruption. *Journal of International Development* 8: 683-96

_____ 1998. Patron-client networks and the economic effects of corruption in Asia. In M. Robinson. ed. *Corruption and Development.* London

Klitgaard, R. 1991. *Controlling Corruption.* London

Landé, C. H. 2001. The return of "People Power" in the Philippines. *Journal of Democracy* 12: 88-102

_____ 1996. *Post-Marcos Politics: a geographical and statistical analysis of the 1992 presidential election.* New York

_____ 1965. *Leaders, Factions and Parties: the structure of Philippine politics.* New Haven

Leach, E.R. 1954. *Political Systems of Highland Burma.* London

Leff, N.H. 1964. Economic development through bureaucratic corruption. *American Behavioral Scientist* VIII: 8-14

Leys, C. 1965. What is the problem about corruption? *Journal of Modern African Studies* 3: 215-230

Magadia, Jose J. 2003. *State-Society Dynamics.* Quezon

Mauro, P. 1995. Corruption and growth. *Quarterly Journal of Economics* CX: 681-712

_____ 1998. Corruption and the composition of government expenditure. *Journal of Public Economics* 69: 263-279

McMullan, M. 1961. A theory of corruption: based on a consideration of corruption in the public services and governments of British colonies and ex-colonies in West Africa. *Sociological Review*: 181-201

Moore, M.P. 1998. Death without taxes: democracy, state capacity, and aid dependence in the fourth world. In M. Robinson and G. White eds. *Towards a Democratic Developmental State*. Oxford

Moscovici, S. 1973. Foreword to *Health and Illness*. C. Herzlich. London

_____ 1982. The coming era of representations. In J.P. Codol and J.J. Leyens eds. *Cognitive Approaches to Social Behaviour*. The Hague

_____ 1984. The phenomenon of social representations. In R. Farr and S. Moscovici eds. *Social Representations*. Cambridge

_____ 1981. On social representations. In J.P. Forgas, ed. *Social Cognition: perspectives on Everyday Understanding*. London

Myrdal, G. 1968. *Asian Drama: an inquiry into the poverty of nation*. New York

Nakata, T. 1978. Corruption and the Thai bureaucracy: who gets what, how and why in its public expenditures. *Thai Journal of Public Administration* 18: 102-28

Noble, T. 2000 *Social Theory and Social Change*. Basingstoke

North, D. 1990. *Institutions, Institutional Change, and Economic Performance*. Cambridge

Nye, J.S. 1967. Corruption and political development: a cost benefit analysis. *American Political Science Review* LXI: 417-27

Parsons, T. 1949 *The Structure of Social Action*. New York

_____ 1951 *The Social System*. New York

Parsons, T. and Shils, E.A. 1951 *Toward a General Theory of Action*. Cambridge, Mass.

Parsons, T. and Smelser, N. 1956. *Economy and Society*. New York

Pedersen, P.E. 1996. The search for the smoking gun. *Euromoney*. September: 49

Philp. M. 1997. Defining political corruption. *Political Studies* XLV: 436-62

Polanyi, K. 1944. *The Great Transformation*. NewYork

Putzel, J. 1999. Survival of an imperfect democracy in the Philippines, *Democratization* 6: 198-223

Radcliffe-Brown, A.R. 1930. Applied anthropology. *Australian and New Zealand Association for the Advancement of Science*. Brisbane Meeting

_____ 1952. *Structure and Function in Primitive Society*. London

Reuter Newswire. 1997. Philippines corruption a nightmare – Ramos. January 11

Robinson, J.O. and Shaver, P.R. 1973 *Measures of Social Psychological Attitudes*. Survey Research Centre, Institute for Social Research, Michigan

Robinson, M. 1998. Corruption and development: an introduction. In M. Robinson. ed. *Corruption and Development*. London

Rogow, A.A. and Lasswell, H.D. 1970. The definition of corruption. In *Political Corruption, ed. A,J. Heidenheimer. New Jersey

Rose-Ackerman, S. 1999. *Corruption and Government: causes, consequences and reform*. Cambridge

Sampson, S. 1983. Bureaucracy and corruption as anthropological problems: a case study from Romania. *Folk* 25: 63-96

Santhanam Committee Report. 1964. *Report of the Committee on*

Scott, J.C. 1969 a. Corruption, machine politics, and social change. *American Political Science Review* 63: 1142-1159

_____ 1969 b. The analysis of corruption in developing nations. *Comparative Studies in Society and History* 11: 315-41

Scruton, R. 1997. *Modern Philosophy: an introduction and survey*. London

Sidel, J. T. 1999. *Capital, Coercion and Crime: bossism in the Philippines*. Stanford

_____ 1998. The underside of progress: land, labor and violence in two Philippine growth zones, 1985–95. *Bulletin of Concerned Asian Scholars* 30: 3–12

_____ 1997. Philippines politics in town, district and province: bossism in Cavite and Cebu. *Journal of Asian Studies* 56: 947–66

Singh, G. 1997. Understanding political corruption in contemporary Indian politics. *Political Studies* XLV: 626-638

Tanzi, V. 1998. Corruption around the world. *IMF Staff Papers* 45: 559-594

Theobald, R. 1990. *Corruption, Development and Underdevelopment*. Durham, North Carolina

_____ 1999. So what really is the problem about corruption? *Third World Quarterly* 20: 491-502

Thompson, M.R. 1995. *The Anti-Marcos Struggle: personalistic Rule and democratic transition in the Philippines*. New Haven

Tilman, R.O. 1968. Emergence of black-market bureaucracy: administrtaion, development, and corruption in new states. *Public Administration Review* 28: 440-442

Ting Gong. 1997. Forms and characteristics of China's corruption in the 1990s: change with continuity. *Communist and Post-Communist Studies* 30: 277-288

Toye, J. and Moore, M. 1998. Taxation, corruption and reform. In M. Robinson ed. *Corruption and Development*. London

Treisman, D. 2000. The causes of corruption: a cross-national study. *Journal of Public Economics* 76: 399-457

Tuan, Y.F. 1974. *Topophilia*. Englewood Cliffs

van Klarvan, J. 1970. Die historische Erscheinung der Korruption, in ihrem Zusammenhang mit der Staata- unde Gesellschaftsstrukur betrachet, *Vierteljahresschrift für Sozial- und Wirtschaftschichte* 44: 289-94. [Reproduced as 'The concept of Corruption' in *Political Corruption*, ed. A.J. Heidenheimer. New Jersey. (Trans. P. Hofmann and K. Kurtz)].

Vivanathan S. and Sethi H. 1998. By way of a beginning. In S. Vivanathan and H. Sethi, eds. *Foul Play: chronicles of corruption 1947-97*. New Dehli

Wade, R. 1982. The system of administrative and political corruption: canal irrigation in India. *Journal of Development Studies* 18: 287-328

Waterbury, J. 1973. Endemic and planned corruption in a monarchical regime. *World Politics* XXV: 533-55

Wei, S.J. 1997. How taxing is corruption on international investors? *Working Paper 6030*. National Bureau of Economic Research: Cambridge, MA.

Williams, R. 1999. New concepts for old? *Third World Quarterly* 20: 503-13

Williams, R.J. 1976. The problem of corruption: a conceptual and comparative analysis. *PAC Bulletin* 22: 41-53

Wilson G. and Wilson M. 1945. *The Analysis of Social Change*. Cambridge

Woolgar, S. (ed) 1988 *Knowledge and Reflexivity*. Sage: London

World Bank. 1997. *World Development Report*. Washington, D.C.

Wurfel, D. 1988. *Filipino Politics: development and decay*. Ithaca

Yang, Mayfair. 1994. *Gifts, Favors and Banquets: the art of social relationships in China*. Ithaca

———— 2000. Putting global capitalism in its place: economic hybridity, bataille and ritual expenditure. *Current Anthropology* 41: 477-509

———— 2002. The resilience of *guanxi* and its new deployments: a critique of some new *guanxi* scholarship. *China Quarterly* 170: 459–76

Zinn, D. 2001. *La Racconandazzione: clientelismo vecchio e nouvo*. Donzelli: Roma

INDEX